I0009799

WORLD BANK DISCUSSION PAPER NO. 432

Telecommunications and Information Services for the Poor

Toward a Strategy for Universal Access

Juan Navas-Sabater
Andrew Dymond
Niina Juntunen

The World Bank
Washington, D.C.

ISBN: 0-8213-5121-4
ISSN: 0259-210X

Juan Navas-Sabater is a Telecommunications Specialist in the Global ICT Department of the World Bank. Andrew Dymond is a Rural Telecommunications Consultant and Managing Director of Intelecon Research (Canada). Niina Juntunen is a former Telecommunications Consultant at Epstar (Finland).

Library of Congress Cataloging-in-Publication Data has been applied for.

CONTENTS

FOREWORD

The significant social and economic impact of the information and communications revolution and the threat of a widening digital divide as a key dimension of poverty, have prompted policy-makers and development institutions worldwide to take measures to ensure that all have access to communications, information, and ultimately knowledge.

Extending the underlying telecommunications and information infrastructure to reach the poor is now acknowledged as one major dimension of the fight against poverty, in which the World Bank Group undoubtedly has a key role to play.

Under liberalized conditions, the telecommunications market has proved remarkably effective in extending the communications network to large territories, including in many instances, poor rural and remote areas. However, the effectiveness of the market does continue to be limited by commercial considerations. While providing service to rural and remote areas can be viable in the long run, commercial opportunities need to be leveraged in the short run by policy and regulatory measures, as well as public financing mechanisms.

The Bank Group's new strategy for the information and communications technologies sector identifies support for universal access as a key strategic direction. Through advice and technical assistance on policy measures, and by providing targeted and selective financing that leverages substantial private investment, the Bank Group supports developing countries in their efforts to curb the growing digital divide.

This paper outlines the multiple dimensions of universal access, describes the different policy, regulatory, and financing mechanisms to combat it; and discusses alternatives for Bank Group support based on specific country conditions. It comes at an opportune time as the Bank is re-defining its vision to respond to the new challenges posed by the information and communications revolution and the digital divide.

We hope this paper will be both informative to members of the Bank Group and our development partners in understanding the centrality to the development agenda of the universal access issue, as well as useful in implementing specific operations in this area.

Mohsen Khalil
Director
Information and Communications Technologies Department

ABSTRACT

Access to information and communications technologies has become crucial to a sustainable agenda of economic development and poverty reduction, and yet access remains concentrated in a few regions and population groups, with the contours of this new 'digital divide' closely following and supplementing existing income and economic divides. However, technological innovations, economic pressures, and regulatory reforms are making access to information and communications technologies more affordable and providing opportunities to close the digital divide.

This discussion paper outlines a number of policy and regulatory measures, including incentives to attract investors to high cost or challenging areas, that can be used under different scenarios to close the digital divide. While Bank Group experience shows an increasing number of projects with specific universal access components, this paper proposes alternatives for Bank Group support for universal access policies, through an appropriate mix of technical assistance and investments.

ACKNOWLEDGMENTS

This discussion paper was made in part possible by financing from the Finnish Trust Fund, which supported a consulting contract with Omnitele (now Epstar) to conduct the underlying research and draft vast portions of the paper. In addition, the team would like to acknowledge the valuable suggestions, feedback and support received from our World Bank Group colleagues, both within the Information and Communications Technologies Department, and beyond. For their particular contributions and active participation in the discussion sessions, we would like to give our special thanks to Björn Wellenius, Rob Schware, Kerry McNamara, Mohammad Mustafa, Eloy Vidal, Vivien Foster, Carlos Braga, Emmanuel Forestier, Randall Riopelle, Charles Kenny, Christine Qiang, Yann Burtin, Peter Smith, Ritin Singh, Paul Noumba, Gaiv Tata, Suzanne Smith, Antonio Estache, Veronique Bishop, Reza Firuzabadi, Pierre Guislain, and Mohsen Khalil. Special thanks also to Anupama Dokeniya and Markku Kääriäinen (Epstar) for their support in redrafting some sections of the paper, and to Andrea Ruiz-Esparza who provided editorial assistance.

EXECUTIVE SUMMARY

Universal Access and Poverty Reduction

Access to information and communications technologies has become crucial to a sustainable agenda of economic development and poverty reduction. Communications technologies affect poverty reduction through three primary mechanisms: increasing the efficiency and global competitiveness of the economy as a whole with positive impacts on growth and development; enabling better delivery of public services such as health and education; and creating new sources of income and employment for poor populations.

Access to communications networks however, remains concentrated in a few regions and population groups, with the contours of this new 'digital divide' closely following and supplementing existing income and economic divides. The 'digital divide', as measured by indicators such as telephone penetration and number of Internet hosts exists not only between developed and developing countries, but also within countries, between urban and rural populations, and between the rich and the poor. While differences in telephone density are very large, these are even more pronounced for the Internet. Of 143 million estimated Internet users in the world, 90 percent are in high-income countries while only 1 percent is in Africa. Two major dimensions of this digital divide are poverty and isolation, measured in terms of disparities between rich and poor on the one hand, and disparities between urban and rural/remote areas on the other. While both dimensions are equally critical, isolation poses major challenges to service expansion, which is why rural communications are central to any discussion of universal access.

General Trends

Technological innovations, economic pressures and regulatory reforms are making access to information and communications technologies more affordable and providing opportunities to close the digital divide. Technological innovations have resulted in falling prices of electronic equipment, convergence between telecommunications, computing, and the media, and the explosion of the Internet. Low cost wireless solutions, ranging from multi-access radio to cellular to fixed-wireless, and increasingly satellite, are now available for rural areas at affordable prices. Business innovations such as pre-pay options or virtual telephony have reduced the entry price at the lower end of the market, and coverage is often available in areas where the fixed telephone infrastructures are poor.

An important trend is the emergence of community access to both basic and value-added communications as a key means of achieving universal access. While individuals in many poor locations may not be able to afford the upfront and recurrent costs of owning a telephone line or an Internet-enabled PC, a community as a whole may be able to effectively share such facilities. Thus, the basic concept of universal access is applicable not only to basic telephony but also to value-added services, such as the multipurpose community telecenter (MCT) model, which provides access to various services, including basic telephony, computing and Internet access, among others.

Options for Expanding Access

Two related issues need to be addressed when designing strategies to promote universal access to information and communications services: the first relates to the 'market efficiency gap', and the second to the actual 'access gap'. The market efficiency gap denotes the difference between the current level of service penetration and the level achievable in a liberalized market, under a stable regulatory environment. The access gap, on the other hand, denotes those situations where a gap between urban and rural areas continues to exist even under efficient market conditions, since a proportion of the population (relatively large in developing countries), cannot afford the market prices at which the service is offered.

The market efficiency gap can be closed with a well-known set of policy and regulatory measures. These include the introduction of competition in all service segments and geographic areas, private provision of service (including privatization of the incumbent), developing a transparent and nondiscriminatory regulatory environment and supporting the creation of independent regulatory authorities, capable of promoting a level playing field and enforcing the service commitments of both incumbents and new operators alike. No direct public financial investment is required to close the market efficiency gap.

However, in order to close the 'access gap' in challenging, uneconomic areas or to reach isolated poor customers, governments may need to employ a mix of several possible approaches. Experience shows that many of these areas can be profitable in the medium term, when private operators are involved and given a fair and transparent regulatory regime. Regulatory incentives to attract investors to high cost or challenging areas can be created through specific universal access policies and public investment subsidy schemes. Such strategies of public support can maximize their impact by leveraging competitive private investment through minimal and well-targeted subsidies ('smart subsidies') to achieve good social returns and commercial viability in the long run.

A wide range of options exist for closing the access gap, which are very dependent on specific country conditions. The paper presents a country classification methodology, based on a number of geoeconomic and policy factors, as well as an approach to selecting the most appropriate policies and financing schemes in accordance with specific country conditions.

Toward a Strategy for Universal Access

The primary instrument used in Bank Group operations to narrow the digital divide has been, and will continue to be, policies and investments aimed at bridging the market efficiency gap. This involves, among others, support to the liberalization of the telecommunications market, the creation of a pro-competitive legal and regulatory environment and the privatization of the incumbent operator.

However, recent Bank Group experience shows an increasing number of projects with specific universal access components aimed at bridging the access gap. Most of these are too recent and have therefore not yet produced a consistent set of monitorable results. However, the initial successes of a small number of projects, such as in Peru and Guatemala, to name a few, have spurred interest in the universal access fund model, which is now the focus of many other operations, some of which go beyond the pure technical assistance approach typical in these early operations and propose sizable investments to support these new policies.

Bank Group support for universal access policies can therefore be provided both through technical assistance and investments, aimed at the design and implementation of universal access regulatory and funding mechanisms. Such a Bank Group strategy for universal access would focus on achieving universal access through a mix of policy reform and targeted pro-poor investment instruments along the following four major strategic directions:

- Design and implement the most *appropriate policies and regulatory instruments* to promote universal access, addressing both the market efficiency gap and the access gap.
- Mobilize financing for *investments* and transactions in access facilities and networks, both from the government subsidy perspective, as well as from the private operator perspective.
- Build *institutions and human capacity* in borrowers to adapt, implement, and make best use of ICTs.
- *Pilot new approaches, create and disseminate knowledge*, and raise awareness within the Bank Group and with borrowers, partners, and the public in general.

1   TELECOMMUNICATIONS, INFORMATION AND POVERTY REDUCTION.

1.1   Knowledge and Development

Access to information, and ultimately knowledge, plays a crucial role in improving the living conditions of the poor[1]. Information and communications technologies (ICTs), in particular telecommunications and information services[2], as tools for access to and processing of information, are therefore key to poverty reduction.

Access to telecommunications and information services, and to ICTs in general, provides crucial knowledge inputs into the productive activities of rural and poor households; makes large regional, national, and even global, markets accessible to small enterprises; and increases the reach and efficiency of the delivery of government and social services. Furthermore, access to ICTs gives the poor a voice, with which they can influence the decisions of policy-makers, and allows them to participate in the decision-making process.

However, there are wide disparities in access to ICTs both among and within countries, a notion which has come to be known as the "digital divide". Narrowing these access gaps and removing barriers to information dissemination, and access to knowledge is therefore a priority in promoting sustainable development and alleviating poverty.

This paper explores the role of ICTs in narrowing the digital divide, and outlines policies, regulatory measures, and targeted investments that the World Bank Group can promote through its operational work in the ICT sector, for improved impact in countries' efforts to reduce poverty.

1.2   Role of Information and Communications Technologies in Poverty Reduction

Telecommunications and information services, and ICTs in general, have a positive impact on poverty reduction efforts through a variety of mechanisms, as discussed below.

ICTs promote integration of isolated communities into the global economy. The predominance of ICTs in all aspects of economic activity in the global economy means that failing to develop technological capabilities relegates countries, regions, and communities to exclusion. A well-developed telecommunications industry, for instance, promotes trade and influx of foreign direct investment (FDI), as shown in the diagram below. Global businesses, no matter their size, are more likely to establish themselves in countries that offer telecommunications infrastructure and facilities that provide them with global reach.

ICTs promote productivity gains, efficiency and growth. ICTs contribute to economic growth by making both global and domestic operations more productive and efficient, equally in the private and public sectors, promoting growth. Indeed, it can be shown that the incomes of the poor grow faster in telecommunications-intensive economies, as illustrated in the following chart: in the last few years, a faster growth in the income of the poorest 20 percent of the population has

---

[1] World Development Report, *Knowledge for Development,* The World Bank, Washington DC, 1999.
[2] While throughout the paper we will often refer to ICTs in general, from telecommunications to computers, or from broadcasting to the postal sector, the primary focus of the discussion will be on the telecommunications sector specifically, as a major contributor to widespread penetration of ICTs.

been experienced by countries where the telecommunications sector is delivering its full potential to the economy, that is, where sector revenues account for 2 to 3 percent of GDP.

Figure 1.1. FDI Flows are higher in telecom-intensive economies

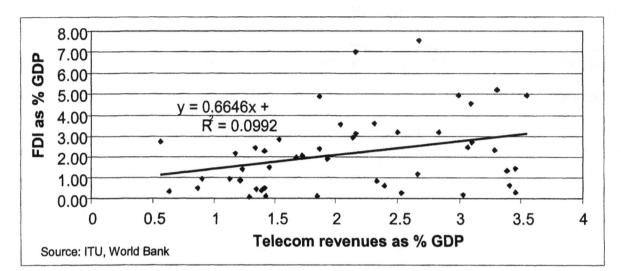

Source: ITU, World Bank

ICTs improve the delivery of public services. As outlined in the ICT chapter of the Sourcebook for Poverty Reduction Strategy Papers (PRSP Toolkit)[3], ICTs improve the overall efficiency of governments and increase the effectiveness of services such as health and education. For example, a number of sources are quoted as showing that students with access to the Internet perform better than students without access, and that every dollar invested in ICTs multiplies almost threefold in terms of improved productivity of the public sector. Furthermore, ICTs extend the reach of public services to the remotest areas, and allow information to flow in both directions, thus effectively empowering the poor and giving them a voice.

Figure 1.2. Income of the poor grows faster in telecom-intensive economies

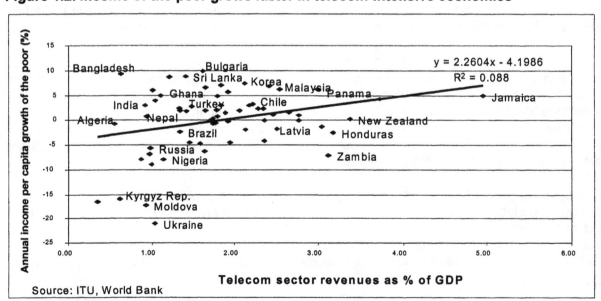

Source: ITU, World Bank

---

[3] See http://www.worldbank.org/poverty/strategies/sourctoc.htm.

ICTs are particularly important for rural and isolated communities. ICTs allow small-scale enterprises, cooperatives, and farmers to obtain accurate information on fair prices for their products and to access regional and national markets. ICTs also reduce the cost of transportation and support the local tourist industry, as shown in Saunders *et al.*[4]. By bringing markets to people rather than forcing people to leave in search of markets, ICTs stem urban migration and generate greater income and employment potential in rural areas, which is one of the most valuable contributions ICTs can make to addressing poverty.

1.3   The Digital Divide

Falling prices of electronic equipment, convergence between telecommunications, computing, the media, the postal sector, and the development of the Internet, coupled with public policies that foster competition and private investment, have increased the possibilities for providing more widespread access to communications services.

However, while some countries and regions have increasing access to these services, other countries and regions are marginalized from the prospects of growth and development because of this lack of access.

This 'digital divide' has two major dimensions, at the international level, between countries, and at the national level, within countries. It is general practice to illustrate the extent of the digital divide *between countries* in terms of penetration of services, such as the telephone, compared to the income level of the country as a whole, as shown in the following figure.

Figure 1.3. Telephone penetration as a function of GDP per capita

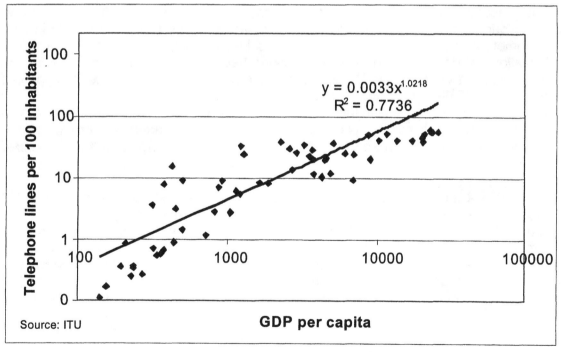

Source: ITU

The equation shown on the figure is $y = 0.0033x^{1.0218}$ with $R^2 = 0.7736$.

---

[4] Saunders, Warford & Wellenius, *Telecommunications and Economic Development*, World Bank, Washington DC, 1994.

As we will see in the next chapter, the gap is even wider if expressed in terms of access to more advanced services, such as the Internet, and by some measures it could be widening every year: while in 1997 the number of Internet hosts per 1,000 people in OECD countries was roughly 50 times larger than in Sub-Saharan Africa, by 1999 this ratio had risen to 70.

Regarding the digital divide' *within countries*, rural inhabitants can be more than 100 times less likely than their urban counterparts to have access to a telephone. In addition, the poor, regardless of location, have less access to communications services than their income level would appear to justify (see the following table).

Table 1.1. Teledensity in selected countries by income level and urban/rural location

Country	Poorest quintile	Quintile 2	Quintile 3	Quintile 4	Wealthiest quintile	% of urban households with telephones	% of rural households with telephones
Nepal	0	0	0	0.5	11.0	10.38	0.11
Panama	1.7	11.0	27.5	51.5	73.8	57.45	9.27
South Africa	0.6	4.7	14.7	33.3	75.0	45.66	4.71

Source: LSMS Surveys[5], The World Bank.

However, many studies show that affordability and willingness to pay are not such large barriers as was previously thought: wherever they are given the choice, poor communities often spend on communications as much as urban communities, in terms of percentage of available income. Kayani and Dymond[6], for instance, point out that "rural communities spend between 60 and 125 percent of their national average, in relative terms, on telephone service".

1.4   The World Bank Group's Strategic Role

Aware of the important impact telecommunications and information services have in reducing poverty, the World Bank has been very active in this sector, supporting governments in their efforts to promote competition and private sector-led investments, with the guidance of the Bank's Operational Policy for the Telecommunications Sector, OP 4.50, issued in 1995, now retired and substituted by the Good Practice statement accompanying the recently approved World Bank Group ICT Sector Strategy Paper[7]. In addition, the Bank has been promoting and engaging in investments in information technology both in the private and the public sector. As a result of these operations, many countries have achieved impressive growth in the telecommunications sector, increased productivity of the private sector, as well as enhanced delivery of public services.

However, the explicit target of these operations has not always been to reduce poverty, but rather to improve the performance of the markets. There is no doubt that liberalization and privatization lead to market efficiency, to growth, and hence, benefit the poor in the long term. However, there is some perception that the benefits of these reforms take too long in reaching the poor. Some studies even appear to indicate that, while in absolute terms the population as a whole is better off, the gap between the rich and the poor may continue to widen in certain areas even after the reforms are introduced, particularly in rural and peri-urban communities where the vast majority of the poor live.

---

[5] See http://www.worldbank.org/lsms/

[6] Kayani, R. and A. Dymond, *Options for Rural Telecommunications Development*, World Bank Technical Paper No. 359, Washington DC, 1997.

[7] World Bank, *Sector Strategy Paper – Information and Communications Technologies*, September, 2001.

The recognition that these communities do not always benefit automatically from these sector reforms, has prompted several developed and developing countries to implement explicit pro-poor policies, some of which have proven very successful in providing universal access to telecommunications and information services. The central objective of these policies is to provide access to services at the community rather than at the individual level. If individuals cannot afford a telephone line or a PC hooked to the Internet, by pooling demand, the chances are higher for the community as a whole to afford such services. Where the community is too isolated for services to be commercially viable given that community's affordability level, there are a number of schemes that allow for targeted subsidies to be used without distorting the market.

An increasing proportion of the Bank's telecommunications sector reform portfolio, in line with the general trend towards country-level poverty reduction strategies, includes in one form or another, a universal access or rural telecommunications component. Although it is too soon to evaluate the results of these new efforts, there is general agreement that, while it is important to make explicit efforts to target the poor, there are various ways of doing this within the general objective of market-driven development. This calls for a better understanding of what types of policies work best under different types of situations.

2   OVERVIEW OF THE ACCESS PROBLEM

2.1   The Two Dimensions of the Access Problem

In terms of access to both basic telecommunications and information services, developing countries have huge disparities between:

- rich and poor, and
- urban and rural/remote areas.

These two primary dimensions of the digital divide can be labeled separately as *poverty* and *isolation*. There is of course a great deal of overlap between them. When we consider possible strategies and solutions however, from the perspective of cost of service provision, the scale of the rural challenge is much greater than that of addressing the problem in poor urban areas. The urban poor, despite being largely without private telephone or information services, are not geographically isolated and can be 'reached' more readily through normal business approaches or access strategies if markets are liberalized.

Rural areas on the other hand often suffer neglect with or without liberalized markets, because they are perceived as carrying both higher risk and lower returns to investors. They are naturally the last to be served, unless some form of intervention is applied.

2.2   The Two Access Gaps

The challenge of expanding the telecommunications network in developing countries to reach the whole population, needs to overcome two separate 'gaps'. These are often referred to collectively, without distinction, and sometimes confused, as "the access gap", but they are different problems, which require different solutions. These gaps are:

- the market efficiency gap, and
- the access gap, *per se*.

The **market efficiency gap** refers to the difference between the level of service penetration that can be reached under current plans and conditions, and the level one would expect under optimal market conditions. This gap can be closed without public financial aid, through sound market-oriented policies in which the private sector plays a leading role in investing in the network and providing services, markets are liberalized, telecommunications operators enjoy a stable regulatory environment, and entrepreneurs are free to profit from providing public services.

Many countries have made impressive progress in closing this gap, through privatization, market liberalization, and fair regulation, as shown later and pointed out in the PRSP Toolkit[8] and elsewhere. However, in implementing such reforms there will always be questions, such as, what are the market's limits, and how to establish optimal regulatory and investment conditions in a less than ideal environment, which need to be addressed on a case-by-case basis.

---

[8] See http://www.worldbank.org/poverty/strategies/sourctoc.htm.

The **access gap** exists because the market has limitations and we reach what we have termed the "affordability frontier". Beyond this frontier, there may be areas or groups that cannot be reached commercially, even in the most efficient of markets, without some form of intervention. Even in these instances, such intervention can be energized and complemented by competitive market forces through the use of minimal and well-targeted subsidies ('smart subsidies'), which can be leveraged to achieve good social returns, and often commercial viability in the long run. The alternative policies and instruments available to address this gap are introduced later.

The following diagram illustrates this conceptual framework: in terms of residential customer penetration, the current telecommunications network of most low-income countries reaches only a small portion of the economic and geographic spectrum. In both dimensions – poverty and geographic isolation – there are huge gaps today.

Figure 2.1. Conceptual access gap framework

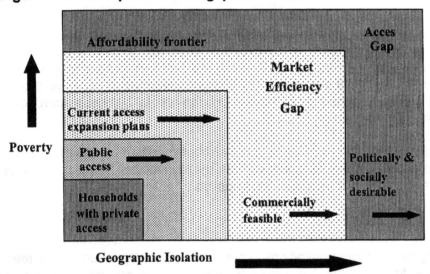

However, access can be extended well beyond the limits of private residential penetration. For example, pay phones are a key access tool, while in rural and poor neighborhoods many private phones are also shared (e.g., the village chief, a businessman, clinic, or government official allows people to make, and often pay for, personal calls).

A further level of access will be reached when current plans or targets are reached in the next few years. This frontier, however, will rarely coincide with the affordability frontier, if set arbitrarily by a government body, since it is often constrained by policies that discourage operators, or new entrants, from reaching optimal service levels or using the most appropriate or innovative retailing methods. There is usually *much more* affordability among rural people to support telecommunications services if those services are accessible. A previous Bank publication on rural telecommunications[9] describes explicitly the basis of this conviction.

The other two levels of service depicted in the diagram represent the levels that may be achieved once the two gaps introduced above are bridged, as a result of a combination of policies, as described later. It is important to stress at the outset however, that despite the apparent sequentiality of the description, the policies used in bridging both gaps deliver the best

---

[9] Kayani R., and A. Dymond, *Options for Rural Telecommunications Development*, Technical Paper No. 359, Washington D.C., 1997.

results if carefully applied in parallel, taking special care that the access gap policies do not preempt perfectly viable market-based solutions.

2.3   Basic Access Indicators

There is no genuine indicator for 'access' to the telephone or telecommunications network, which can be applied universally or consistently across countries. The indicators used throughout this paper, though inadequate, can be discussed in combination, sometimes with the assistance of judicious assumptions to present a picture of the situation around the world.

TELEDENSITY

The most readily available statistic is 'teledensity', expressed as telephone lines, also known as direct exchange lines (DELs), per 100 people. This is traditionally mapped against GDP per capita, as illustrated in the previous chapter. The International Telecommunications Union (ITU) publishes regularly these curves showing a fairly predictable relationship between teledensity and national income, as was discussed above, with the poorest countries having teledensities of less than 1 percent and the richest countries with well over 50 percent.

Given the rapidly increasing numbers of mobile telephony subscribers, which in a large number of countries have overtaken the number of fixed telephony subscribers, teledensity statistics often are expressed as a combined figure of fixed and mobile subscribers per 100 inhabitants.

RESIDENTIAL PENETRATION

It is more meaningful to separate business and government lines (usually all of these are classed together as 'business' lines) from residential lines and to calculate residential telephone penetration in terms of lines per 100 households. This more accurately describes the level of penetration reached among the general population, as it takes the sociocultural factor of average household size into consideration. It often reveals more graphically the disparity between rich and poor countries, since the national networks of poorer countries usually have a higher proportion of business, government, and institutional lines. The following diagram offers an approximate view of typical household penetration from low to high income countries.

Figure 2.2. Universal access and universal service

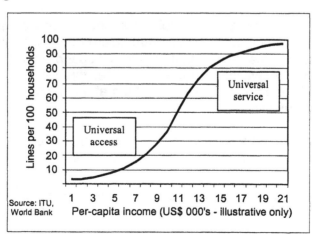

The diagram also introduces the concepts of 'universal service' and 'universal access', which will be discussed later. Broadly speaking, in the OECD country context, with residential penetration typically above 75 percent, households without a telephone are considered to be disadvantaged. Hence advanced country governments and regulators are concerned with policy instruments for achieving universal service – service to every home.

In low-income countries, however, the only realistic objective is to achieve 'universal access' whereby every citizen would be able to access a public phone in every community, neighborhood, village, or vicinity[10]. Therefore, access strategies for low income countries are important to address the problem of low affordability, as described below.

AFFORDABILITY

Countries, regions, households and individuals of all income levels spend somewhere between 1 percent and 3 percent of their income on telecommunications. A good approximation is 2 percent. Whereas some of the poorest countries of the world spend less (low income countries average 1.2 percent) as shown in the following graph, many poor countries spend more than 2 percent. For example, the African average is 2.0 percent, with many countries above this.

Figure 2.3. Telecom revenue as percentage of GDP

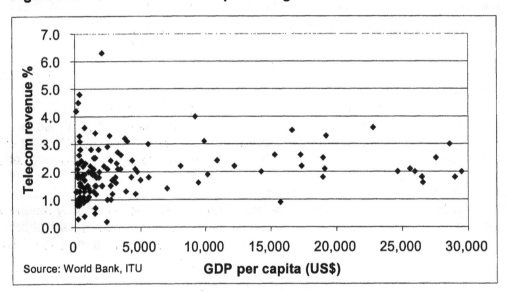

Source: World Bank, ITU

Although the vast majority of people in developing countries – and poor people everywhere – do not have a telephone in their home, there is a great desire to use the telephone *if it is available*. There is increasing evidence that shows that people will spend up to 2 percent of their income on phone calls if a phone is available to them. Hence, this percentage can be taken as an indicative average to estimate how much a household at any income level can afford to spend annually on telecommunications.

Telephone tariffs – particularly the balance between line installation charge, the monthly rental, and local and long distance call charges –vary a great deal around the world. This of course

---

[10] A similar public access approach is now being followed in many countries, including developed economies, in attempting to universalize access to the Internet and other advanced services.

tends to dictate whether or not people can afford a private phone, and impacts the volume of usage, but does not necessarily influence the percentage of income spent on the telephone. Telephone affordability can thus be represented by a curve which reflects 2 percent of family income distribution (the Gini curve), as shown in the figure below, indicating affordability across the population. Household telephone penetration will largely depend on tariff levels, as to whether the 'entry level' tariff[11] is within a households' affordability.

Figure 2.4. Peru household affordability

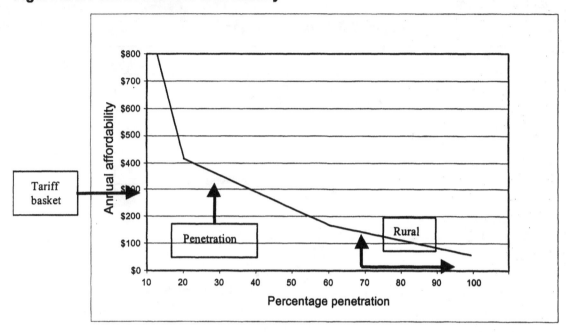

The graph assumes that telephone service is normally provided to the richest segment of society first, progressing to lower income groups as penetration increases. The curve illustrates the specific case of Peru. Residential penetration, now at 30 percent, is unlikely to pass 40 percent in the near future because household affordability below the distribution's fourth decile falls below the tariff basket.

In the case of Peru, 30 percent of the population is rural. If we assume that these also correspond to the lowest 30 percent in the income distribution curve, we can see that they will generally not be able to afford private lines unless special tariffs are designed for them. They will thus depend on public phones and other public means of access.

Peru is a good example to illustrate the challenge and unique features of rural service provision in a liberalized environment. With liberalization, tariffs are usually 'rebalanced' to reflect costs more closely. Rental and local call charges tend to rise while long distance and international charges reduce. In Peru, the $300 cost of the basic tariff basket is now clearly beyond the affordability of the poor, whereas lowering long distance call charges will make it easier for them to make a few calls to relatives and contacts in the city. Thus their dependency on public phones as the only feasible alternative has increased, while their ability to make productive use of public access vehicles has also increased.

---

[11] Can be defined in varying ways, for instance, as a basket consisting of one year's monthly rental charges, a typical number of local calls and 10 percent of the connection fee.

Rural and urban telephone statistics are usually either unavailable or untrustworthy, especially for developing countries. ITU statistics show the percentage of a nation's telephone lines located in the main city. This only hints at the disparity between urban and rural areas. If we assume conservatively that 80 percent of all the telephone lines outside the largest city indeed serve other smaller urban areas, as opposed to villages and rural locations, we can estimate the scale of the problem[12]. Disparities between 20:1 and 60:1 are common, as implied by the following diagram[13].

Figure 2.5. Urban-rural gap

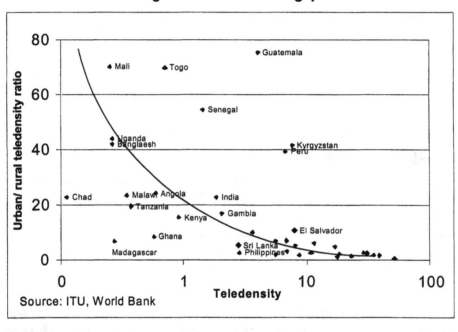

As an example, very few of Tanzania's villages (average population 2,500) have even a single telephone. Estimates by Bank staff showed the disparity to be around 25:1, which is lowerthan that predicted by the 80/20 assumption. This situation is not uncommon in Africa. The few communities that have a business or a government office with a phone, or a working pay phone, attract users from far and wide, often prepared to walk or ride for hours to get to the phone. People – many of them very poor - tend to show by cases such as these that they want and need access to the telephone.

India also illustrates this point. Only half of India's villages (average size 1,000) have a phone. Because of low penetration in rural and poorer urban centers, India's own brand of phone shops (known as "STD PCOs") are an almost ubiquitous phenomenon in roadside communities or businesses. Many other countries from South Africa to Thailand have seen similar tele-businesses arise to serve rural populations, the urban poor who cannot afford their own telephone, or the traveler.

---

[12] The ITU published some time ago. some data for 1996 showing percentage of telephone lines in urban areas. However, methodological problems with the source of the data may have been the cause why the ITU discontinued this data series, and therefore more recent information of this type is not available.

[13] This graph only *illustrates* a situation, which the authors know to be the case, from many visits to developing countries. The assumption that 80 percent of telephones outside the capital are in urban locations is an estimate (and very conservative in many cases). Even if a reasonable average, it is most likely incorrect in most cases. Because of the inherent inaccuracy of this or any methodology to estimate the situation, the graph should not be used to infer reality in the case of individual countries.

2.4   Access to Information Technology and the Internet

The disparities noted above in access to basic telecommunications services are magnified in terms of access to the Internet and to information technology. The ITU has only recently begun to publish country statistics on Internet hosts, service providers, and users, as well as availability of PCs and modems, illustrating the magnitude of the digital divide.

The number of Internet service providers, hosts. and users is now growing in many developing countries at the same pace or faster than in advanced countries, albeit from a very low base and very unevenly. For example, of 325 million estimated Internet users in the world[14], over 80 percent are in high-income countries while only 1 percent are in Africa, as shown below[15]:

Table 2.1. World Internet statistics

Region	Total users (k)	% of world	users/ 10,000
U.S. and Canada	108,054	33.2%	3,538
Latin America	12,936	3.9%	249
Europe	89,984	27.7%	1128
Asia	103,544	31.8%	293
Oceania	7,565	2.3%	2,500
Northern Africa	307	0.1%	22
South Africa	2,400	0.7%	549
Rest of Africa	550	0.2%	8
Total	325,339	100%	547

Source: ITU, 2000 data

While virtually all countries in Africa now have at least one Internet Service Provider, almost 90 percent of the Sub-Saharan African market is in South Africa and more than 99 percent of all users are in main urban centers. To address this situation, some countries have made the decision to provide local call Internet access across the country. Furthermore, a few are using similar policies to promote access to the Internet as those used for promoting access to the telephone, namely a universal access fund, as described in Chapter 4.

Data on the availability of PCs and Internet access within developing countries with a rural-urban breakdown is anecdotal or not readily available. This makes it difficult to know the degree to which the poor, including in rural areas, are without access to modern information services. However, the affordability barrier is even more steep in this case, given the important levels of investment required on the user side to even get started (PC, modem, telephone line, ISP connection charge), in addition to the recurrent costs involved.

Therefore, in this realm public access has even more relevance, in relative terms, than in the case of basic telephony, as will be discussed later. This has been shown by some studies[16],

---

[14] 2000 statistic published in April 2001by ITU.

[15] About 65 of the 103 million users in Asia are in Japan, Korea, Singapore, Hong Kong and Taiwan.

[16] See NTCA, *Initial lessons learned about private participation in telecenter development*, and TeleCommons Development Group, *Rural Access to ICTs – The challenge for Africa.*

where an increasing prominence of public modes of access to information and communications has been documented around the developing world, in different forms, ranging from basic phone shops to full-fledged multipurpose community telecenters.

3 TECHNOLOGY AND MARKET SOLUTIONS FOR THE ACCESS GAPS

Recent technological advances, rapid cost reductions, as well as market innovations, have created many opportunities for increasing access to ICTs in rural, remote and poor urban areas. While declining costs of equipment and service are making ICTs generally more widely accessible, new technologies are overcoming the constraints of location. Rural and remote areas, where setting up wireline infrastructure would not be economically viable, can be served through alternative, wireless means, including via satellite. Similarly, market retailing innovations and community access are bringing telecommunications and other ICTs within the reach of areas that cannot afford individual household access. These trends are discussed below in turn.

3.1   Technology and Cost Trends

WIRELESS AND SATELLITE TECHNOLOGIES

The wireless explosion – cellular, personal communications, 'wireless local loop' and satellite systems – are having a spill-over effect on poor urban and rural areas. The number of cellular subscribers is currently growing at 30 percent to 50 percent per annum around the world, and at 150 percent in Africa. This is a direct result of both liberalization of this segment of the market, and a steady decline in prices of wireless equipment. Privatization of incumbent mobile operations, combined with new competitive entry by private operators, has had a spectacular effect. Prices of mobile telephony are tumbling, pre-pay options have reduced the entry price at the lower end of the market, and coverage is often available in areas where the fixed telephone infrastructure is poor.

In an increasing number of countries, mobile telecommunications services are achieving substantial penetration. In some cases, mobile services substitute for fixed line service. The following figure indicates the wide range of situations world-wide. Similar effects are found in both low-income and high-income countries. The variations observed within these two groups are often accounted for more by regulatory differences and market timing, rather than by fundamental demand economics. For example, Uganda's cellular operators are allowed to grow at the expense of the fixed line operator whereas in India, cellular operators are handicapped by very high license fees, and relatively low competing tariffs in the fixed network.

The use of cellular phones as village 'mobile pay phones' has been clearly demonstrated in Bangladesh, India, Morocco, and elsewhere, which illustrates the principle that wireless technology is making a difference to some rural areas. However it must be recognized that such developments are often still only at the margins and do not yet represent radical change for remote and rural heartland areas[17].

Wireless local loop systems, also known as fixed-wireless technologies, are specially designed products used by some operators to rollout service rapidly and efficiently in suburban and peri-urban areas, and are also being used to serve rural communities. Although it is not necessarily the case that wireless solutions are less expensive than wire-based solutions, some countries

---

[17] In Bangladesh, approximately 1,100 mobile village payphones have been franchised to private operators under a special financing program by Grameen Phone. However, Bangladesh has close to 60,000 villages without telephone service. See Cina Lawson and Natalie Meyenn, *Bringing Cellular Phone Service to Rural Areas*, World Bank Viewpoint Note No. 205, March, 2000.

have chosen to license specific wireless local loop operators as a way to take advantage of these technologies in a competitive environment.

Figure 3.1. Mobile substitution effect

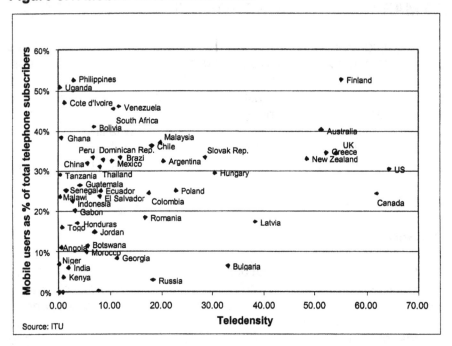

Source: ITU

DECLINING COSTS

Low cost wireless solutions, ranging from multi-access radio to cellular to fixed-wireless, are now available for rural areas. Advantages of wireless systems over traditional wired solutions, apart from lower cost beyond 5km radius from the telephone exchange, is that they can be relatively easy and rapid to deploy, avoiding the complex process of laying cables, and managing and maintaining them properly. This 'last mile' problem can often be the weakest link, and the least well managed in the whole telecommunications infrastructure.

Some wireless systems can be implemented for between $500 and $1,000 per line in suburban and peri-urban areas, though the average cost in rural areas is still more typically in the $1,500 to $3,000 range and often considerably higher, depending on population density, terrain, and whether solar power panels are required. The need for special repeaters, towers and solar power systems can easily double or triple the installed cost over that of the equipment.

Satellite systems – particularly very small aperture terminals (VSATs) – are now reaching the point where they are a serious technology option in more remote areas. Chile, Colombia, Ethiopia, Guatemala, Kazakhstan, Peru, South Africa, Thailand and other countries have all made sizeable investments in VSAT technology. Whereas the cost of the equipment can be as low as $3,000 to $4,000 for two or three village phone and fax lines, the final installed price (like the case of wireless) may be two or three times this amount.

VSATs can be also integrated with small wireless systems to extend the reach of individual terminals to customers and villages in the local vicinity and thus to serve them more economically than with additional VSATs or with wire-based 'last mile' connections. Almost all VSAT suppliers now either have their own wireless systems, or strategic alliances with wireless suppliers, or are in the market looking for an 'acquisition' to secure their position. Their motivation is to be able to deploy hybrid VSAT/wireless solutions in distant rural communities with demand for up to 50 subscribers, at prices competitive with the $1,000 per line of suburban wireless systems.

Another kind of VSAT – an 'asymmetric' terminal which can deliver broadband signals, including voice over IP, in one direction with low to medium speed in the return direction – can be deployed widely to extend high speed Internet access and telecenters to rural communities.

The result of these developments is to create a shifting balance of opportunities increasingly dominated by innovative wireless solutions. Actual boundaries between technologies depend to a great extent on:

- distance from the customers to the main network;
- potential customer density; and
- the type of service (e.g., just telephony and fax, or data and Internet also).

Figure 3.2. Typical market niches for various technologies

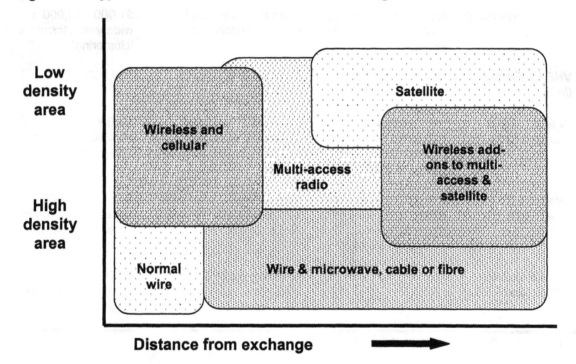

The following diagram illustrates the typical market niches in just two dimensions, showing the technology most likely to be chosen within the context of varying distances from an existing telephone exchange (x axis) and varying subscriber densities (y axis).

It will be noted that 'wireless and cellular' and 'wireless add-ons' are eating into the market niche formerly dominated by other technologies. Multi-access radio is an example of one technology which has to adapt by lowering prices drastically and adding wireless for the 'last mile' in order to survive even as a rural technology.

The various applications and typical per-line costs to reach rural or peri-urban areas are summarized in the following table. This can be indicative only, since costs are very dependent on local factors and especially on the power source.

Table 3.1. Technology cost guidelines

Technology	Density / Application	Geography / Distance from telephone exchange	Cost range per line (in econ. niche) incl. Accessories
Cable direct from urban switch	high and clustered (sub-urban or peri-urban communities)	Max 5 to 10 km radius from exchange	$250 - $1,000
Rural exchange or concentrator with wire network	low/medium and clustered (small town or large village with good affordability)	as above, may serve clusters (e.g., 100 subscribers) located more than 10 km from nearest exchange	$1,000 - $2,000 including trunk system and building
Fixed cellular and wireless	Medium/high, not clustered	Medium area (<30 km radius per cell)	$500 - $1,500 heavily dependent on users per cell
Multiaccess radio	low but clustered (e.g., more than 5 users per location)	Wide area (radius of (several hundred km)	$1,000 - $5,000 varies widely with terrain and 'clustering'
VHF/UHF single links	low, no clustering & no satellite alternative	Medium-long distance (>25km)	$10,000 +
Satellite VSAT (stand-alone)	low, but most economic with some clustering (e.g., justifying 2-3 lines)	very large area, long distances (>200 km)	$3,000 - $8,000 plus $0.05-0.10/min 'space segment'
Integrated VSAT/WLL	low, but serving larger distant communities or clusters (typically 10 to 50 lines in vicinity)	large area, but economic at shorter distances (e.g., 100 km)	$1,500 - $3,000 plus $0.05-0.10/min 'space segment'
Mobile satellite (MSAT and LEOs)	low, with no clustering	very large area & long distances	$1,000 - $3,000 plus $0.50/min space segment'

Source: updated from Kayani and Dymond (1997)

3.2   Retailing Innovations and Community Access Trends

RETAILING INNOVATIONS

Declining prices, and new technological offerings have combined with both retailing innovations and policy mechanisms to make access to communications services more widespread. Two separate but interrelated development streams – one market driven and the other policy driven – are emerging in the business of providing access to information and communications services, as represented in the following diagram:

Figure 3.3. Retailing innovations

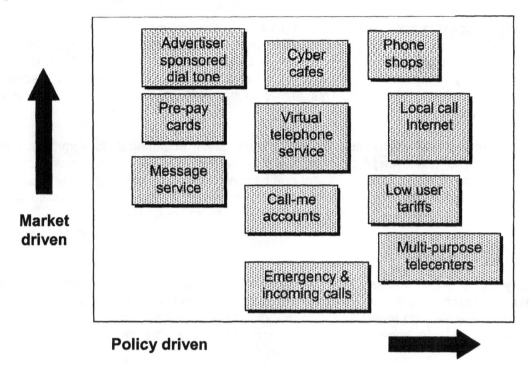

Some of these services have the following characteristics:

- *Use of revenue-enhancing features inherent in digital telephone systems:*

  For instance, messaging and 'virtual telephone' service concepts allow users to have their own telephone number and to receive and transmit messages from any telephone, or from public access phones, by means of a PIN-based account or security code, without actually having to 'own' a telephone line. Botswana, Brazil, and South Africa are examples of countries already implementing this concept.

- *'Pre-pay' technology extends the market to lower income users:*

  Pre-paid cards purchased anywhere (e.g. within a phone shop, from general stores, kiosks or from 'same brand' phone shops elsewhere in the country), allow people to control their expenditures, or more well-off people to buy call units for their relatives to use, at the same time simplifying operators' collection systems and indeed guaranteeing collection. Pre-payment is accelerating mobile penetration into a mass market, including among lower income groups, throughout the world and is now being experimented with also for fixed line service in South Africa and elsewhere.

- *Some schemes are primarily policy-driven in support of low-income users:*

  For instance, reverse-charge 'call me' facilities, activated by PINs, can be used to allow poor or rural people to call collect to their relatives, from private or public phones. Special low-use tariff packages or 'emergency number only' facilities have mostly originated first in advanced countries (e.g., in the EU) under universal service initiatives. At least some of these can be applied appropriately in developing countries.

COMMUNITY ACCESS TRENDS

Community access, as opposed to private access, to the whole range of ICTs is emerging as a popular solution that makes good sense developmentally, and is also good business. By focusing on providing public access, be it to a telephone line, to a radio, TV screen, or to an Internet terminal, countries can aggregate demand so that a large number of people benefit from one or a few connections. This allows sustainable provision of services even where incomes are low.

This trend is gathering momentum as markets liberalize. In Senegal, for example, more than 6,000 privately operated and highly profitable telecenters have come into existence since the early 1990s and public access to a telephone has more than doubled. India, Peru, South Africa, and Thailand have also seen dramatic growth in privately owned and operated telecenters providing rural inhabitants with new information sources and opportunities.

Pay Phones

The pay phone is the simplest and most common means of extending access. Well placed pay phones can reach large segments of the population who do not have private telephone service, as well as generate high revenues for operators. Rural pay phones can be profitable since they are often the first telephone to arrive in a community and attract the 'affordable market' of the whole community.

However, statistics for pay phone use around the world reveals another disparity, as the higher-income and more highly developed countries typically have achieved higher pay phone penetration than lower income countries, as shown in the figure below.

Although lower income and lower penetration countries have the greatest need for public pay phones, the general challenges to telecommunications infrastructure rollout – including market domination by an inefficient and unmotivated incumbent – impede the public as well as private facilities. Pay phone liberalization – licensing of special pay phone operators – has been one way of accelerating this form of access deployment. Ghana and Peru are two examples where this has taken place successfully in developing countries.

Figure 3.4. Payphone penetration as indicator of access

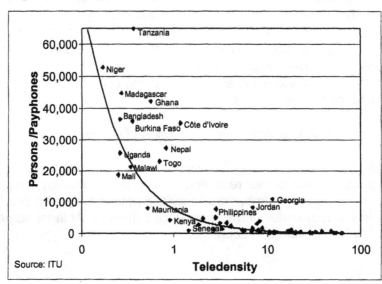

Telephone Shops

Serious problems with money collection, vandalism, and general maintenance exist with pay phones in developing countries, especially in their rural areas. One means of addressing this has been with card phones. However, the most successful solution for rural areas is to place pay phones with business people or 'phone shop' operators to mind the phones for profit.

'Public call offices' usually operated by the national state-owned PTT have been the traditional form of manned access provided to the population at large. However, this has barely scratched the surface of what is both technically feasible and economically viable. Every continent now has interesting examples of how private tele-businesses have emerged to show how both the market efficiency gap and the access gap can be bridged. They are bringing acceptable, culturally appropriate and commercially viable service to the urban and rural poor as part of a public service portfolio that is valuable to users across the whole socioeconomic spectrum.

Card pay phones, phone and fax shops and various combinations of the two are sprouting around the world. Their generally successful financial performance reinforces the point made earlier that people in most places, irrespective of their economic level, are usually willing to spend a portion of their available income on information and communications services for personal or business purposes.

Telecenters

From the basic case of a phone shop adding one or two PCs and Internet access to its service portfolio, to the mainly urban cyber-café to the full-fledged multi-purpose community telecenter (MCT) complete with multiple PCs, Internet access, media services, computer training and business services, among others, the telecenter is the ultimate example of community access strategies.

The concept first emerged in developed countries of Western Europe, North America, and in Australia, in regions where rural isolation, lack of purchasing power or low quality telecommunications facilities were seen to hinder participation in the information economy. Hungary was the first country in Central Europe to develop a large number (over 100) of rural 'telehouses' with a range of ICT equipment. Brazil has also piloted the European model while other countries such as Bangladesh, India, Indonesia, Peru, and South Africahave independently developed simpler models. The latter have commenced in urban or larger rural communities that have a low level of private telephone penetration and/or a large enough market for public access businesses to be commercially viable. At the moment there are pilots underway in a large number of countries.

Examples of Community Access Initiatives

The following table provides only a sampling of the cases known to us of the above described trends:

Table 3.2. Some examples of community access initiatives

Country	Description
Bangladesh	1,000 'mobile pay phones' operated as revenue sharing businesses by women with the assistance of microloans by Grameen Bank

Ghana	Several hundreds of village phone shops operated as revenue sharing businesses
India	'STD PCOs' and 'teleports' offering phone and fax services are virtually ubiquitous in cities, towns, and main road communities and villages. Small franchised telecenters (e.g., in Tamil Nadu) are also emerging.
	3,000 village based 'mobile pay phones' operated as personal revenue sharing businesses in the states of east and west Uttar Pradesh, promoted by cellular operator Koshika Telecom. At least three other Indian cellular operators also developing mobile pay phone businesses.
Indonesia	5,000+ 'Wartels' are franchised multiline pay phone shops in cities and towns throughout the country, many more less formal 'telekiosks' in neighborhoods and smaller communities, and 2,000+ 'Xpress Connection' VSAT-based revenue sharing businesses in remote villages.
	Some Wartels have also added Internet access to their service offerings.
Morocco	Over 6,000 private 'Teleboutique' pay phone shops are virtually ubiquitous in cities, towns and roadside communities, one third in rural areas.
Peru	Rapid growth of telecenters includes commercially operated and franchised 'monocabinas' in rural areas, which offer phone, fax, and PC with Internet connection.
Senegal	Over 7% of main telephone lines are privately run phone shops. A new program aims at encouraging the addition of Internet service.
South Africa	Wide range of fixed line and cellular based phone shops, some franchised businesses (e.g., 'Mr. Phone') and others less formal, in townships and rural communities.
Thailand	Village heads and store owners provide public phone businesses as agents of the PTT operator
Uganda	Mobile and second fixed licensee, MTN operates a network of franchised phone shops, some with PCs and Internet .
Zimbabwe	General store owners, clinic administrators and government agents with private business lines operate informally as public call offices

The common denominator in all of these is that individual private operators see business opportunities in public services and the regulatory regime allows local reselling to take place. A much larger number of countries have implemented traditional PTT rural pay phone programs, many of which have proven to have good demand, but fail to remain fully operational and viable due mainly to poor maintenance and, in an unmanned model, the lack of individuals with a business incentive to mind the operations.

Policy Implications of Telecenters

Unlike the telephone access gap, for the moment there is little chance that the Internet access gap can be readily closed on a purely commercial basis, even in the most liberalized of market conditions. Hence the concept of public-private partnerships to design and fund community telecenters has emerged as an urgent and attractive means of making tools of the information society widely available.

Multipurpose community telecenters (MCTs) lately have received much attention from many international development agencies and other players in the development community, as potential vehicles for a wide variety of social and development services, beyond purely expanding access to ICTs. Services delivered through MCTs include: education and health services, financial and business development services, market information and access services (in particular aimed at enhancing the productivity and profitability of agricultural activities and small businesses), etc.

However, there are some challenges with telecenter development – especially for MCTs – that need to be taken into account:

- *Commercial sustainability:*

  While many MCTs have the *potential* to be self-sustaining in the medium to long term, in the early stages almost all require large amounts of public investment to offset the high start-up costs and piloting of new ideas. Many receive support from aid agencies and community and technology partners. At the moment, almost all MCTs combine public involvement with 'an eye' towards eventual commercial sustainability or profitability.

  However, only one third of UK telecottages achieved financial viability after several years, while another 40 percent were barely self-supporting. In other countries (e.g., Canada and the USA) telecenters receive public support for strategic reasons related to business and community development, skills training, etc. In developing countries, though, MCTs could be more sustainable in the long term, because they serve a higher percentage of people and businesses without their own private facilities.

- *Potentially harmful competition with commercial businesses:*

  Phone shops are a commercially viable access business. Owners can also afford to add fax, PCs and Internet service in many cases – thus migrating into a telecenter-type business – as local demand, availability of good quality access circuits, telecommunications tariffs, and finance allow them to. This 'bottom up' approach is likely to be more self-sustaining, although it may not fulfill all of the development benefits imagined for telecenters.

  On the other hand, the proliferation of 'top down' purpose designed, publicly funded and basically 'free' telecenters may compete with otherwise viable businesses, by drawing away basic telephony and fax revenues and hindering the growth of independent ICT access business. Policymakers thus need to consider whether it would not be more appropriate to support a program consisting of micro-loans to help develop and scale-up currently successful independent businesses or franchises, combined with regulatory reform at the national level to promote appropriate tariff regimes and universal Internet access strategies.

- *Information sources and local dependency:*

  Some studies have suggested that the greatest developmental impacts are achievable first of all from familiar and basic communication media, including telephony and broadcasting. This would thus support the 'bottom up' strategy discussed above. Under this scenario MCTs should only be implemented in concert with the creation and development of local information sources and Internet skills (e.g., web site and database creation).

Considering all of the experience thus far, and emerging issues, it is our view[18] that sustainable development of telecentres needs to be approached from three converging directions:

---

[18] Similar views are expressed by Proenza in his recent article on telecenter sustainability (Proenza, 2001).

- regulatory initiatives to remove barriers to entry by private sector service providers and to encourage both the rollout of affordable and suitable quality Internet service outside the main urban centers, and the use of appropriate technologies such as wireless or VSATs by access providers;

- bottom-up development approach, in which small businesses such as phone and office service shops are encouraged to develop an advanced ICT component in response to market opportunities, perhaps with the inducement of micro-loans for investment in PCs and Internet access; and

- business-community partnerships under appropriate conditions, with international donor or NGO assistance, complementing rather than competing with successful small phone shop and telecenter businesses.

4   POLICY AND REGULATORY MODELS FOR IMPROVING ACCESS

4.1   Introduction

Both technology and commercial entrepreneurship are favorably impacting the market, as we have seen, and slowly widening the reach of telecommunications networks. However, policy and regulatory interventions will continue to be crucial in addressing both access gaps in developing countries.

Privatization, liberalization, an effective regulatory framework, and efficient regulatory institutions, are key elements in a strategy to address the market efficiency gap. In addition, a variety of regulatory and funding options can be deployed to close the access gap, which is likely to remain in developing countries even under efficient markets due to lower purchasing power in poor and rural areas.

This chapter reviews a wide range of policy and regulatory options, trying at the same time to highlight best practice examples. The different policy and regulatory options are presented with reference to applicable country conditions, in terms of degree of liberalization and geographic and economic features of the country, since ICT infrastructure costs differ greatly depending on the geographic, topographic, and demographic characteristics of the country, and the achievable level of market penetration and access also depends on regulatory, economic, and geographic dimensions.

4.2   Country Groupings Based on Liberalization and Geoeconomic Dimensions

A two dimensional *descriptive* model was developed to classify countries in terms of their degree of telecommunications liberalization thus far and their level of geoeconomic challenge. Altogether, 62 countries were analyzed and studied, and their main characteristics from the universal access perspective summarized in Annexes 1 and 2. Seventeen of them where profiled in more detail, as presented in Annex 3.

The model shows four degrees of market liberalization and three levels of geoeconomic challenge, which might affect decisions on specific liberalization strategies (especially for rural areas) and other policy options available.

DEGREE OF LIBERALIZATION

The first dimension of the model is the degree of liberalization, divided into four stages:

- monopoly environment in fixed and mobile services,
- monopoly in fixed but competition (or at least duopoly) in mobile services, and most often also in other market segments, such as value-added services and sometimes pay phones,
- partial liberalization, where only some segments of the fixed telephony market remain under monopoly provision, often domestic long-distance and international telephony, and
- fully competitive environment.

DEGREE OF GEOECONOMIC CHALLENGE

This dimension reflects the degree of geographic and economic challenge. Geographic challenge reflects the ratio of remote and challenging rural areas compared with the total surface area of the country. Economic challenge describes the income level and the level of economic disparity in the country. Four basic indicators were used to derive the level of geoeconomic challenge:

- GDP per capita (the higher the lower the challenge),
- gini index (economic disparity, the larger the index, the more challenging) ,
- ratio of total land per arable and crop land (reflecting the possibly mountainous or deserted areas and with sparse population), and
- geographic size (area) of the country

A combined geoeconomic challenge rating was calculated from these four basic indicators. The methodology is described in Annex 4.

While low income countries will always be more challenging than high income countries, because the level of teledensity they can economically achieve is lower, countries at all income levels have both highly profitable, marginal and loss-making situations. The geoeconomic challenge rating thus relates to whether the market can achieve a level of access to the poor and to under-served areas which is appropriate to a country's overall level of affordability. In a high income country, achieving 100 percent household penetration may be the appropriate target, whereas in a poor country, providing public access within reasonable walking distance of everyone might be a more realistic goal. In this context, severe inequality of income, large geographic size and unfavorable distribution of population or land, present real challenges to telecommunications service providers and regulators at whatever level of access a country's government deems to be appropriate.

Based on the rating previously described, a three-level challenge classification was derived:

- *Group 1: uniform, densely populated and/or small country*

  A country with little regional variation because of small size, high population density and/or topographic simplicity. Rural and urban differences, however, might still be high, with regard to both population density and economic inequality.

- *Group 2: significant regional variation*

  A country with major regional variation, with some regions providing significant challenge for the telecommunications cost structure due to geographic extremes. The country's economic inequalities may also be significant.

- *Group 3: remote and challenging areas*

  Typically the size of the country is large and topography is challenging (mountainous or islands) and thus requires special technology and investments to provide service coverage. Economic disparity between geographic areas is extreme.

Based on the two dimensions just described, each country can be placed visually within a grid showing their current status, as illustrated in Table 4.1 below[19]:

Table 4.1: Country categories on liberalization and geoeconomic dimensions

Liberalization/ Challenge rating	Monopoly	Only mobile competition	Partially liberal	Open market
GROUP 3 Remote areas and/or high economic disparity	Nepal ▶	Burkina Faso Chad Kenya ▶ Mozambique Niger Senegal South Africa	Angola Bolivia ▶ Brazil ▶ China Indonesia Mali Mauritania Nigeria ▶ Russia Tanzania Venezuela[20] ▶	Argentina Australia Canada Chile Colombia Madagascar Mexico Peru U.S.
GROUP 2 Significant variations	Gambia Nicaragua ▶	Botswana Bulgaria Cote d'Ivoire Ecuador ▶ Jordan Morocco Romania ▶	Ghana Honduras India ▶ Kyrgyz Rep. Sri Lanka Thailand	Dominican Rep. Finland Guatemala Malaysia Philippines Uganda
GROUP 1 Uniform, densely populated and/or small country		Gabon Greece Hungary ▶ ▶ Latvia Malawi Slovak Rep.	Bangladesh Poland ▶ Togo	El Salvador Georgia New Zealand UK

▶ indicates that the country is moving toward the next liberalization stage in the near future. A double arrow indicates that the scale of change will amount to a 'leapfrogging' of one stage.

4.3 Policy and Regulatory Options for the Market Efficiency Gap

The first step to begin fulfilling the communications needs of the poor is to leverage the full potential of market mechanisms in reaching out to poor communities, by fostering a competitive, private sector–led market. There can be dramatic increases in access to telephone and Internet services through a telecommunications sector reform program based on three pillars[21]:

---

[19] This table is compiled with information that is deemed to be correct to the best of the authors' knowledge at time of writing. The situation in particular countries with regard to the liberalization degree may have changed since.

[20] Throughout the text we will refer to the "Republica Bolivariana de Venezuela" as simply "Venezuela".

[21] These will only be summarily treated in this section, since they do not constitute the major focus of this paper.

competition, independent regulation and private sector operation.

Provision of service by private operators in the telecommunications sector improves teledensity and profitability of the business, through efficient operation, more investment, and lower cost of capital, among other reasons. Countries with private provision, especially if coupled with competition, also see a higher level of employment in the sector in the medium term, despite a widespread belief that privatization may trigger significant unemployment.

Competition improves performance, through faster and more efficient line rollout and bringing prices closer to the actual costs of service provision, thus improving service affordability and enhancing access to services. In the reformed telecommunications markets of Latin America, for instance, basic line rollout grew approximately three times faster than in countries with a state monopoly and twice as fast than those with private monopolies. A liberalized telecommunications sector is also vital to make access to advanced information technology more affordable, because a large part of the costs of Internet access are accounted for by telecommunications. In Africa, for instance, countries with a highly liberalized telecommunications network had costs of Internet access eight times lower than those with closed markets[22].

However, real competition is largely dependent on the effectiveness of the regulatory agency in creating a level playing field for all operators, and requires the regulatory environment of the telecommunications industry to be conducive to a well-functioning competitive market. This can be achieved through legal and regulatory mechanisms that promote, among other things: fair and non-discriminatory interconnection between telecommunications operators; cost-oriented tariffs, and the elimination of internal cross-subsidies; as well as recourse to a strong and truly independent regulatory agency, capable of enforcing rules. Regulators also have the challenge of creating market-oriented incentives that make service provision to poor and rural areas commercially viable. Even rural areas can become an attractive business under liberal entry and incentive policies, as proven by the example of Chile[23].

4.4   Bridging the Access Gap in a Less than Liberalized Environment

In this section we discuss regulatory actions which have been used to bridge the access gap in an environment of monopoly provision of fixed line service, independently of the existence or not of mobile competition. However, it must be pointed out that, while these interventions have, in some countries, proven successful during the initial reform process, accelerated liberalization is generally recognized as far more effective in reaching universal access goals.

SERVICE REQUIREMENTS

In some countries the privatization conditions have included granting of a significant exclusivity period for the incumbent, as in South Africa and Mexico (elapsed in 1998). The rationale for the exclusivity period has been to let the newly privatized incumbent meet the universal service obligations unhindered by competition. During the exclusivity period, access expansion is taken

---

[22] See infoDev, UNECA, *Internet Economic Toolkit for African Policymakers*, World Bank, 1999.
[23] See Björn Wellenius, *Extending Telecommunications Service to Rural Areas – the Chilean Experience*, World Bank Viewpoint Note No.105, February, 1997. It is important to note that many rural areas were served without requiring a subsidy, since the incentives offered, such as stable regulation and radio frequency licenses along with the service licenses, were sufficient to attract commercial entrants.

care of with incumbent rollout or service requirements[24] and/or specific regional targets. Sometimes the continuation or extension of the exclusivity period is linked with the incumbent's success in reaching the rollout targets. In South Africa, if the incumbent meets its build-out obligations, an additional year of exclusivity is offered. As will be discussed later, service requirements must be very carefully designed to avoid over-provisioning and crowding out of potentially more efficient new entry.

However, even when the monopoly operator is capable of reaching its targets, introducing competition has always shown that it can improve the efficiency of line rollout and bring prices closer to the actual costs of service provision, thus improving service affordability and better enhancing access to services throughout the country. The tandem exclusivity-obligations will always be a second best compared to liberalization, and, if at all warranted, experience shows that the exclusivity period should be limited to no more than 2-3 years.

Service requirements can be presented in the form of:

- rollout targets for private lines,
- teledensity targets,
- targets for public facilities such as pay phones or phone shops,
- quality of service levels,
- targets to reduce waiting list, or
- minimum time to fulfill requests for a mainline.

Such requirements can be included in the licenses of new entrants as well as incumbents, so as to encourage network investment in high-cost and peripheral areas. The most spectacular results from such a policy thus far are found in Hungary, where both the incumbent and new regional monopolies received very stringent rollout targets, including for rural areas, which they have essentially met, and are approaching market saturation at the prevailing tariffs. Box 4.1 summarizes the lessons learned.

REGIONAL MONOPOLIES

In some countries, monopolies have been regional, rather than national, and have predated reforms or been established during the reform process to support rural network development. The regional operators can be either state-owned, as in Brazil prior to 1998, privatized as in Hungary and Argentina (during the monopoly period), or co-operatives where communities act as shareholders, as in Bolivia. At the dawn of liberalization, consolidation and strategic alliances often take place between the regional, frequently small sized operators.

PUBLIC-PRIVATE PARTNERSHIPS

Schemes which involve the private sector, and may thus help to accelerate network rollout, but which essentially perpetuate and prolong monopoly dominance include build operate transfer (BOT), build transfer operate (BTO) and similar arrangements. These are revenue sharing schemes between operators and private sector participants. Private participants finance projects and provide operating expertise for the agreed time period. In some Asian and Latin American

---

[24] For the purposes of this paper, by requirements we mean all the conditions that are written into the license of an operator, regardless of whether they were mandated by the regulator or the result of a voluntary commitment by the operator in an open bidding process.

countries this approach has been adopted to extend network coverage in challenging and remote areas. In Indonesia, for instance, five western-backed companies known as KSOs were licensed to install fixed telephone lines in five geographical regions, operate them for 15 years and, at the end of the contract term, transfer ownership to the incumbent. However, this scheme has not worked well in practice due to an imbalanced revenue sharing agreement and difficult recourse to independent mediation, which has prompted the private operators to negotiate an early exit.

Box 4.1. Lessons learned about service requirements

Fairness: Service requirements should be fair for all players and commercially feasible. Unrealistically ambitious requirements may jeopardize the operators' financial performance and their ability to meet the targets. In Malaysia, only the incumbent has service requirements, but it is requesting similar requirements to be placed on other four operators, to achieve the high network penetration goals set by the government (50 lines per 100 inhabitants).

Clear scope: Based on country-specific criteria, the regulator must clearly state which operators are subject to service requirements. There are increasing examples where mobile operators have rollout requirements, for example: the Philippines, where mobile operators must provide fixed or semi-fixed wireless lines; South Africa, where mobile operators must provide public pay phones, or Morocco, where the second GSM license includes build-out requirements into rural areas. Balancing the requirements and the operator capacity to reach them is however critical, and it is also important to make sure there is enough breathing room for competition to take place effectively.

Specificity: It is important that service requirements be specific enough to be enforceable, covering delivery time and areas to be covered, among others. If geographic objectives are not explicit, the high-cost areas are easily left unserved. In many cases, the rural service requirements are specified as targeting service to all villages or regional centers of a certain size, e.g., villages with more than 500 inhabitants. In the Philippines, for example, the licenses with rollout targets did not specify where rollout should take place and the government's objective of one rural line per ten urban lines was not met as operators concentrated on lucrative areas and business customers. In addition, solid enforcement procedures to follow up the actual accomplishment of committed targets and a plan of sanctions to be imposed in the case of failure are a must if license conditions are to be met.

Service targets as bid evaluation criteria: Using build-out targets as a bid evaluation criterion in competitive bidding processes, in addition to the bid price, encourages new entrants to commit themselves to rollout targets that may be higher than the regulator had set as minimum requirement, and in addition will be more feasible than if the regulator tries to fix them upfront. Examples of this are Uganda, where the Second National Operator's bid evaluation criteria included a network rollout plan in addition to the bid price; Kenya, where similar bid evaluation criteria were used in the award of a mobile cellular license; India, where the regional local fixed operator bid evaluation criteria gave some weight to rural coverage plans (albeit only 15 percent), Brazil, where a similar approach was adopted. However, potential difficulties or delays in reaching the goals they had promised, makes it a risky strategy to select the winners based purely on promised rollout targets, which is why in most cases analyzed the evaluation criteria consisted of a mix of financial and rollout criteria.

Potential pitfalls: Service requirements can be counter-productive encouraging massive internal cross-subsidization, if the targets are not set in a market-oriented manner and are not adjusted to the country or area specific characteristics, such as cost of line installation, limits on technology deployment, or affordability of service. For example, in the Philippines, large unused capacity resulted from high fixed line build-out obligations imposed on mobile operators; in South Africa, very high residential churn rates (as high as 75 percent) were experienced because private residential service was not affordable for low-income households compared to public access.

Some countries have undertaken smooth liberalization strategies, where, even when the incumbent is granted exclusivity, provision of value-added services, such as data transmission, Internet access or 'virtual telephony', for instance, is liberalized. These services can have an important demonstration effect about the benefits of competition. Liberalization of the public retail access markets, by allowing the resale of basic service, including provision of pay phones, phone shops and telecenters, constitutes a very effective strategy to begin liberalizing the sector, and at the same time provide the instruments for improved access to services by the poor.

A second market segment that tends to be liberalized early is the mobile market. Countries that have followed this path include Kenya, Morocco, South Africa, Tanzania, and many Latin American countries. Increasingly, in countries with poor fixed infrastructure, mobile service is acting as a substitute to basic services, despite the higher service charges, when the incumbent is incapable of meeting demand. In China, in the vast regions of the north where basic services are lacking, the demand for mobile and paging services is growing rapidly despite the very high prices compared to income levels. Generally, however, liberalization of the mobile sector also forces operators to bring tariffs closer to costs, which brings obvious benefits to subscribers.

Moving towards full liberalization, governments may decide to liberalize all fixed line market segments at once, or only a subset initially. Partial liberalization in some less developed countries means that only the local loop is liberalized, at least in theory, and highly profitable long-distance or international long-distance remain under monopoly. This is due to the unbalanced tariffs and the incumbent's interest in protecting the revenues gained from national and international long distance traffic. However, in addition to the fact that local competition has not proven easy to introduce in practice, this form of partial liberalization perpetuates unbalanced tariffs, the existence of a dominant player in the market and, in general, suboptimal network development and service provision.

4.5   Bridging the Access Gap in a Liberalizing Environment

There is room for both the incumbent and new entrants to succeed in the market, especially in a situation of large unmet demand. Removing barriers to market participation will accelerate network expansion, but only if the regulatory environment is such as to provide stability for private investors. With carefully planned mechanisms, rural penetration can be substantially improved by introducing competition in different service segments and geographic areas.

EMPHASIS ON PUBLIC ACCESS

Public access to telecommunications services forms a focal part of universal service/access plans and policies. In addition to low income levels and low telephone usage in rural areas, the line installation costs in challenging areas can be so high that the private line becomes impractical as a target for most of the population. By providing public access, a large number of people benefit from one or a few lines. From the operator's point of view, pay phones and telecenters provide higher revenues compared to residential lines and, when strategically situated, the operator is able to achieve commercial viability. An additional motive to emphasizing public access is that once the initial network infrastructure is in place, the network expansion is less expensive if the demand exists, for example in the business sector.

As noted above, in some countries virtual telephony has been an innovative step towards increased access to telecommunications services for the poor. Virtual telephony gives a subscriber a telephone number and a voice mailbox, enabling him or her to receive messages and access them from any phone. An upgraded but still economical service, radio paging, would alert the subscriber when new messages arrive.

In addition, as was noted before, provision of public access to Internet and ICTs through enhanced phone shops, cybercafés, or telecenters, is receiving increasingly more attention from both policy makers and entrepreneurs, as the concerns of the widening 'digital divide' are becoming widespread, and as opportunities for new businesses in this area become clearer. Indeed, OSIPTEL, the Peruvian regulator, included the provision of telecenters to midsized communities as part of the package that was auctioned during the 1999 round of bidding for subsidies of the FITEL, and a similar approach is being followed in other countries as a natural extension of the universal access fund model (further discussed below).

REGIONAL OR SPECIAL RURAL OPERATORS

In several countries special rural operators have been licensed, often with the support of universal access fund subsidies, to expand access to high-cost and remote areas where the incumbent has not rolled out its network. By licensing operators to serve specific rural areas, the regulatory agency can select priority locations for enhanced access, to counteract the typical situation that new services are first introduced into major urban centers and only slowly to peripheries and rural communities. Selection of these priority areas is typically done based on socioeconomic dimensions, often first targeting some of the poorest regions (e.g., Peru[25]).

As with regional licensees, rural operators also may have either monopoly concessions (e.g., Bangladesh) or operate in competition with others, usually the incumbent (e.g. Chile, Venezuela). Monopoly rural operators have a certain period of exclusivity before the concession area is opened to competition. In this way the operator has time to build its network and enlarge its customer base before introduction of competition. Bangladesh licensed two rural operators with effective exclusivity several years ago (although their growth appears to have been hindered by regulatory weakness). Box 4.2 below summarizes some lessons learned in this area.

CREATING A LEVEL PLAYING FIELD IN THE LIBERALIZED SERVICE SEGMENTS

Interconnection has a huge impact on new entry, which puts tremendous pressure on the regulatory agency to establish clear interconnection rules. The terms and conditions of interconnection need to be made public and be enforced in a timely fashion to avoid incumbents being able to delay new entrant's deployment. New entrants often have fewer resources and poorer negotiation power and ability to cope with delays caused by interconnection negotiations than the incumbent.

As discussed in detail in Kayani and Dymond (1997), the existence of substantial externalities due to incoming traffic toward rural networks, as well as of differential incremental operating costs between urban and rural networks, would require well thought-out and cost-based

---

[25] For a discussion of the Peruvian model, see Geoffrey Cannock, *Telecom Subsidies: Output-Based Contracts for Rural Services in Peru*, World Bank Viewpoint Note No. 234, June 2001.

interconnection agreements. These might indeed need to be asymmetrical or skewed to some extent toward the rural network operator, to take into account these effects.

Box 4.2. Lessons learned about rural and regional concessions

Packaging lucrative areas with higher-cost areas: This can be a way to ensure balanced network expansion between regions, so that the poorest and most uneconomical areas are not left unserved. To keep operations feasible, concession areas should be large enough to secure sufficient traffic levels. Also, allowing bidders to tender for several adjacent territories, or as many areas as they want, increases the possibilities that all the regions are tendered for. In Chile, for example, some of the most unprofitable areas did not attract any bidder and needed to be re-bid under more attractive terms. When Tanzania was divided into four zones with plans to issue two mobile licenses for each service area, only the Coastal Zone attracted operators, since the other regions did not include major urban centers in them. When Kenya issued tenders for eight regional operators, the initial restriction limiting bidders to no more than two areas were eliminated in response to comments from the market place to allow bidders to combine areas.

Bundling of services and technological neutrality: In order to attract bidders for rural or regional licenses, multiple services may be bundled under one license, but without mandating a specific technology. In addition, the license can give an opportunity to expand operations to other areas in return for enhancing coverage, e.g., the award of a nationwide license tied to widespread population coverage. In Venezuela, for example, the rural licenses allow mobile and multimedia services in addition to fixed access, long-distance and international services. In Uganda, the second national operator license allows the operator to offer mobile services and it is meeting the rollout commitments using a mixture of GSM, fixed wireless and fiber-based facilities. In Chile, pay phone operators have the right to install as many additional private lines as they see feasible, in addition to the pay phone rollout objectives set in the licenses. In Brazil, if either "mirror" licensees or incumbents succeed at meeting their service expansion targets ahead of schedule, ANATEL will free them to enter new service markets ahead of the full liberalization date, set for 31 December 2001.

Preferential access to scarce resources: The efficient exploitation of wireless technologies necessitates a transparent regulatory process in spectrum allocations but, in the case of rural areas, the allocation of frequency spectrum free of charge can be an important inducement to entry. Chilean authorities provided the benefit of guaranteed use of certain radio frequencies along with the licenses in the universal access bidding process.

4.6   Smart Subsidies and Other Financial Schemes to Promote Universal Access

Traditionally, cross-subsidization has been the primary form of financing the provision of universal access, usually under monopoly regimes. In environments where tariffs are not rebalanced, the cost of installing lines in remote and rural areas tends to be subsidized from other, more profitable revenue sources. Initial line connection and rentals are frequently subsidized from tariff revenues, while local call tariffs are priced below cost and subsidized with the revenues from long-distance and international traffic. The use of cross-subsidies, however, does not encourage operators to develop efficiency in rural line provision. This may, in fact, inhibit the motivation to maximize profits and make rural service viable, thereby limiting the ability of operators to effectively expand service.

When markets start to liberalize, a range of special financing mechanisms and investment subsidy schemes are available to attract investors to high cost or challenging areas. Experience is showing that many of these areas can be profitable in the medium term, when private operators are involved and given a fair and transparent regulatory regime. The subsidy element is primarily a market inducement to spark interest and reduce risk in the early years.

COLLECTION OF FUNDS: THE UNIVERSAL ACCESS FUND

In a competitive environment where other operators, in addition to the incumbent, share the universal service/access responsibility, the costs of provision of universal service/access, including rural expansion, can be financed through special funds. Funds are set up as a transitory mechanism[26] to finance network expansion in challenging and unprofitable areas. Universal service/access funds, sometimes called telecommunications development funds, award subsidies to operators, usually in a competitive manner, to make the regional or rural licenses more attractive for the operators.

The fund can be financed from various different sources as summarized in the following table.

Table 4.2: Sources of financing for the universal access fund

Source of Revenues	Definition/Description	Examples
Government budget	Funds provided by government contributions from the Treasury. This is often considered to be more economically efficient than any other mechanism, however, in practice budget allocations risk being dropped in the annual national budget discussion process.	This was the approach used in Chile and planned in the Philippines.
Seed finance by development bank or agency	An initial government contribution to the Fund is financed by international organizations. This "seed finance" in its early stages, enables the Fund to become operational as quickly as possible. Such an approach can be crucial in the poorer developing countries, provided that mechanisms are put in place to evolve to a regular universal access fund.	Recent World Bank projects in Mozambique, Nicaragua and Nigeria, among others include a small portion of seed financing for the universal access fund. Similar schemes are under discussion in other Bank projects.
Licensing or spectrum fees and auctions	Funds come from the sector itself, rather than from the economy at large, through the regulatory process. When spectrum auction proceeds are used, revenues have proved to be highly seasonal and unpredictable.	This was the approach used in Guatemala, where the Fund is financed from 70 percent of the revenues of spectrum auctions.

---

[26] Typically designed to function for a period that ranges between 5 and 10 years.

Operator revenue contribution	All operators are charged a given percentage of their annual gross revenues, often known as the universal service levy. The levy generally varies between 1 and 2 percent (though higher values are not totally unheard of), and participating operators are usually basic service providers, and increasingly mobile operators*.	This is the most common approach, used in Colombia, the Dominican Republic, Peru, South Africa, etc.
Interconnect levies	Incumbent or other designated operator carries a universal service obligation (USO) and raises levies from other operators as incremental interconnection charges, to compensate it for its "access deficit", which is the difference between the costs of the USO and the revenues received. In this case, no fund is created as such, but rather subsidies flow among operators, normally to the incumbent. Such an approach, however, is opaque, and the operator has no incentive to reduce its costs. Especially in the least developed countries where the incumbent is far from providing universal service, open auction subsidies supported by license fees, transparent levies on all telecommunications operators, or government budgets are preferable.	In Malaysia, the incumbent remained the sole universal service provider for an interim period of two years before the establishment of a universal service provision "USP" fund, during which period its costs are recovered via a "USO charge" on all interconnecting traffic.
"Virtual fund" transfers	'Virtual funds' support universal access providers on the basis of a regulator-prescribed costing methodology, with the money flowing directly between operators, rather than through an intermediary. Such an arrangement removes the requirement for a physical Fund administration, and is therefore more efficient, but can be prone to litigation.	This approach is foreseen in UK legislation, but has not been put in place, and is under consideration in Argentina and Mexico.

* The regulatory agency should make a decision whether to impose the levy also on new entrants: for instance, the EU universal service principles call for a moratorium on such levies for new entrants until they reach a minimum market share level of 1 percent.

On balance, while it is economically more neutral to use the general budget, it appears more practical and achievable in low-governance environments to have the telecommunications sector self-finance its own network expansion through small, mandatory contributions by operators. A theoretical argument in favor of this approach is that it will be the existing subscribers – the beneficiaries of the externalities from adding additional users to the network – who finance the expansions in the end. However, in the case of poor low-income countries, funding universal access purely from such a levy alone is unlikely to produce sufficient funds to make an impact in the short run, and the use of government budgetary resources, backed by international finance institutions and other donors, may become necessary initially.

DISTRIBUTION OF FUNDS: "SMART SUBSIDIES" VERSUS "BEAUTY CONTESTS"

A prime regulatory objective is to *minimize* the use of subsidies, which can be achieved through the use of competitive bidding. In such a process, new entrants and sometimes existing operators compete for subsidies for network build-out in certain unprofitable areas, with the subsidy being awarded to the operator with the lowest required subsidy or the highest service rollout commitment, or a combination of both. The allocation of funds collected under one of the schemes described above through such a competitive process is known as "smart subsidies" and is considered the most efficient and effective manner of fund distribution.

The introduction of competition through a bidding process for the use of funds encourages operators to look for the best technology and other cost-savings practices. This tends to minimize the subsidies, if they are required at all. The choice of such funding strategy can also support a level playing field among operators so that none of the operators is overly compensated or unfairly burdened by the funding mechanism.

In Chile and Peru, the mechanism is built in such a way that funds are allocated to the deployment rather than the operation of the networks. The mechanism is market oriented, as interested participants set the level of subsidy through competitive bidding and operators thus bid only if they see a commercial opportunity. In a few cases, some of the most challenging areas did not receive any bids and had to be re-bid. In some of the early processes, bidding for very low subsidies has caused financial problems for some operators in cases where the amount of subsidy bid has been too low (or even zero). This affected the rollout schedule, resulting in service delays, which is why in Chile, the bid evaluation criteria were modified to evaluate bids based also on delivery time alongside the subsidy requested.

An alternative method, also known as "beauty contests", is to distribute funds on application, based on operator development targets, actual investments in uneconomic areas or in special projects, with no organized competitive bidding. In Malaysia, no competitive bidding is organized but the fund compensates operators based on their investments in uneconomic areas. Needless to say, this process may prove less transparent and prone to error and/or interference than an open competitive bidding process.

COST MODELS AND CALCULATION OF MAXIMUM SUBSIDY

In the "smart subsidy" approach, it is important to ensure that the subsidy allocated will not be higher than the social benefit obtained from the implementation of the project. Fund administrators use elaborate economic models to analyze potential projects in terms of their financial net present value and their economic net present value (NPV). Only projects where the economic NPV is positive and the financial NPV is negative are selected and prioritized based on their economic NPV. The maximum subsidy is estimated as the absolute value of the financial NPV. For a description of this approach in the case of Chile see Wellenius (2002).

In order to calculate the financial NPV, proxy cost models are used, similar to the ones common in analyzing interconnection charges and establishing price caps. For a discussion on proxy cost models and their application to interconnection, tariffs and universal service see Laffont and Tirole (2000). The economic NPV takes into account benefits that accrue to the community rather than to the service provider, and are therefore not captured by a pure financial analysis. The simplest approach used in these models to calculate the economic NPV is to take into account the avoided costs in transportation and wasted time to reach the nearest payphone or telecenter.

Annex 5 proposes a very simple model for rapid appraisal purposes, based on general indicators readily available, providing a rough indication of the cost of achieving universal access in the sample countries. The application of the model to the 62 sample countries has also shown that it can be twice more costly on average, on a per capita basis, to provide universal access in countries that have not introduced sector reforms, than in countries where a competitive environment has taken root.

ELIGIBILITY FOR FUNDS

The tendency is that basic service providers, including pay phone operators, and sometimes also mobile operators, are entitled to compete for funds. In Peru, there is some controversy about who contributes to the fund and who is eligible for funding. The incumbent pays the levies, but is not eligible for any funds, despite having universal access targets in its concession.

In addition to supporting operators, funds can be distributed also to help low-income users to afford telecommunications services. Current examples to date are primarily the US and a few EU countries, the reason being that developing countries are primarily concerned with promoting universal access goals, rather than the more ambitious goal of universal service.

FUND ADMINISTRATION

Whenever the universal access policy calls for the creation of a physical fund, the fund can be administered by the national regulator or by an independent body such as the Universal Service Agency in South Africa. Often, when the fund is administered by the regulator, it is still considered to be a separate legal entity, with its own accounting and management, sharing with the regulator only the board and some common administrative services.

The duties of the fund administrator include, among others, the following:

- select and evaluate the geographic areas to which funding will be targeted,
- estimate the parameters that will feed into the model to calculate the maximum subsidy for each area,
- handle the competitive bidding and selection process in an efficient and transparent manner, and
- carefully follow-up the implementation, enforce fulfillment of the obligations and apply sanctions if needed.

OTHER FINANCING OPTIONS: CONCESSIONAL AND MICRO-LOANS

Low interest loans, provided by governments or bilateral and multilateral aid agencies, can be used to encourage operators' network build-out in most challenging regions. This financing method was pioneered in the U.S. through the Rural Electrification Authority (REA) loans which telecommunications operators were also given access to. In developing countries, government budgets are frequently short of funds for telecommunications development programs. However, high-cost areas create large up-front costs for the operators and thus institutional loans to help finance the initial capital investment costs would be useful, especially as generally domestic capital markets in developing countries are weak.

Telecommunications projects usually demonstrate good returns once the project becomes operational, provided the regulatory environment can secure a level playing field for the entrants. Low interest loans are not, however, advised unless these other conditions are also met.

To encourage network utilization, existing operators, possibly with the help of microcredit institutions, can set up schemes to partly finance diverse retail activities. The prerequisite, however, is that the regulatory regime must not prohibit reselling of services. The traditional approach is to franchise a telephone line or a telecenter operation to private individuals or small businesses and to pay a certain percentage of commission to the franchisee. This way, operators can often secure higher revenues than from a public phone because the private incentive tends to keep lines working well. Small loans may also be granted to upgrade services to include fax and Internet services.

As was discussed above, in Bangladesh, Grameen Phone, an operator offering traditional cellular services in urban areas, gives loans through Grameen Bank to low-income women entrepreneurs in rural areas to provide pay phone services based on cellular technology. Community usage drives up airtime, and the entrepreneur is typically able to repay her loan within a few months.

4.7   The Emerging New Breed of "Rural" Operators

The trends in technology combined with the regulatory and financial incentives described above are giving rise to a new generation of telecommunications operators focusing on the rollout of service to rural, remote and low income areas.

These fall into the following general categories:

- *Cellular operators expanding into fixed services*

    Examples of where this has taken place are Western Wireless in Ghana, MTN in Uganda, and three regionally licensed operators in Venezuela.

- *Subsidiaries or affiliates of technology suppliers established as operators*

    Some wireless and VSAT suppliers have formed operating affiliates and gained licenses to provide rural telecommunications services in Brazil, Chile, Colombia, Guatemala, Mexico, Peru, and Venezuela, and may soon have opportunities to bid for licenses in several African countries (e.g. Kenya, Nigeria, and Uganda) and Asia (e.g., Nepal), in addition to other Latin American countries (e.g. the Dominican Republic, and Nicaragua). Their primary motivation was initially to develop new markets for their equipment, but their operating subsidiaries are slowly establishing their independence.

    One very interesting example is Global Village Telecom (GVT), a subsidiary of Gilat Satellite Networks, which has secured rural licenses in Colombia, Chile, and Peru , and a 'mirror operator' license in Brazil.

    Another example is Comunicación y Telefonía Rural (CTR) in Chile, a subsidiary of SR Telecom, the leading Canadian multiaccess and wireless supplier. This company is now established as a viable entity in its own right and will eventually be spun off as a separate operating company.

Direct to Phone International, a subsidiary of STM Wireless, also secured joint ventures to operate VSAT based services in Venezuela (in association with CANTV) and Mexico.

- *Local service providers and joint ventures*

  A number of locally controlled firms or joint ventures with international partners have obtained licenses, for example in Bangladesh, Ghana, Guatemala, Mexico, and Peru.

- *Regional or international joint ventures*

  At least two new ventures into the African regional market are in the process of forming, one a joint venture between a VSAT supplier (Titan Corporation) and an African cellular operator (ORASCOM/Telecel) with multiple licenses and the other a new Canadian and US-financed start-up venture, African Sky Communications.

These cases demonstrate that a wide range of players have an increasing stake in the rural and 'universal access' markets. They are also convinced that profits can be made, at least in the medium to long run.

Box 4.3. New rural operators: experience and outlook

CTR Chile, in a private interview indicated that the experience thus far, although very difficult, has only served to confirm that rural markets can be made profitable given the ingredient of legal and regulatory stability, incentive and secure finance. CTR has recently received a $25 million loan from the IADB and, is meeting its financial objectives. Although it accepted an obligation to install pay phones in 1,800 villages in 9 license territories, CTR has to date installed more than 15,000 lines and believes that the economic potential of its regions is approximately 40,000 lines.

When asked what role the Bank Group could play in contributing to the success of these universal access ventures, three players volunteered the following consensus of requirements:

- Equity participation – typically up to 30 percent by IFC would be welcomed
- Limited or non-recourse debt
- Guarantees, or assistance to secure guarantees, in addition to stable legal and regulatory conditions
- Assistance with up-front 'soft' issues such as market research and expertise
- Support of contentious regulatory matters, such as interconnect and curbing the monopoly tactics of incumbents
- Assistance to governments in helping to define clearly the universal access strategies and mechanisms
- Credit and seed finance (to government) to help establish universal access funds
- Credit to assist with the establishment of telecenters and other experimental retail mechanisms which could develop the ICT markets

On balance, these players are both contributing a great deal to the experience and understanding of rural telecommunications markets, as well as providing an opportunity for partnership.

In several cases, the companies have taken significant risks and faced challenging situations, venturing into businesses which are new to them. With few exceptions, their finance has been through a combination of partner equity, private placement venture capital, and rural access fund subsidies. In a minority of cases, government export credit loans[27], development capital[28], or development bank[29] finance has been made available.

On balance, private entrepreneurial initiative has been responsive to new licensing opportunities. Whereas rural markets are traditionally believed to be unattractive, these cases indicate that they are considered worth the risk to an increasing number of players.

However, according to the views of several of these players, the speed with which their ventures achieve success and commercial security would be substantially improved if the World Bank Group (especially the IFC) played a more active financing role, as described in Box 4.3 above. Possible strategic roles for the Bank Group are discussed in Chapter 6.

---

[27] E.g. Canadian Export Development Corporation
[28] E.g. Commonwealth Development Corporation
[29] E.g. Inter-American Development Bank

5 WORLD BANK GROUP EXPERIENCE TO DATE

5.1 World Bank Experience

The recently approved World Bank Group ICT Sector Strategy Paper and its related Good Practice Statement[30], point out that "The Bank Group supports efforts of developing countries to accelerate information infrastructure sector growth, introduce new services, improve performance, and extend services to more people". The general principles for achieving this are private provision of service, open entry and competition, and government responsibility for policy and regulation, which emphasize competition.

Projects supporting telecommunications sector reform in the mid-90's followed these principles by focusing primarily on development of a stable legal and regulatory environment, privatization of state-owned enterprises and promotion of new entry by private participants. This was already a major change from the previous Bank experience in the sector, in which the bulk of the Bank portfolio was large direct investments in the infrastructure of state-owned enterprises.

This initial approach to implementing the policy was targeted at bridging the "market efficiency gap" we described above, which can itself go a long way in providing services to the poor. For instance, following Bank-supported reforms in Peru, residential telephone penetration among the poorest 25 percent of the population in Lima rose from 1 percent of households in 1995 to 21 percent in 1998[31].

However, the recent OED/OEG review of Bank and IFC activity in this sector from 1993 through 1999, pointed out that this approach did not pay enough explicit attention to a pro-poor agenda. The report pointed to the need to:

- pay more attention to the linkages between telecommunications and informatics and the poverty-reduction agenda; and
- make rural/universal access one of the pillars of the new information infrastructure strategy

The above mentioned Good Practice Statement also indicates that "Services that are deemed necessary for social, development or security reasons, but that are unprofitable even under liberal entry and pricing policies, can be provided to low-income (including rural) population groups through communal facilities (such as telecenters) and/or rendered viable through limited, targeted subsidies". This hints at the possibility of putting in place universal access assistance mechanisms aimed at closing the "access gap". The use of subsidies as a last resort to support the provision of telecommunications services to the poor is acceptable so long as they are clearly targeted at improving access by the poor, particularly in rural areas.

The OED report does acknowledge the fact that the World Bank is lately beginning to implement some explicit support for measures aimed at improving access to information and communications services by the poor, through a new generation of projects which include specific components targeting rural/universal access.

While a uniform approach to assistance in universal access has not yet been established, some trends are already emerging in the World Bank portfolio, summarized in Table 5.1 below.

---

[30] See http://www.worldbank.org/ict
[31] OSIPTEL, 1999.

Table 5.1. World Bank universal access portfolio

Country	Description of the universal access project or component	Status
Bolivia	Technical Assistance (TA) to support rural energy and telecommunications, through eventual creation of a fund: rural fund regulations and operating procedures and procedures for the auctions for rural projects. The project aims at the development of rural telecenter pilot projects, and assessment of results.	Under preparation
Burkina Faso	TA to develop a strategy to improve the connectivity of rural localities using smart subsidy schemes.	Under preparation
Cambodia	With funding from The Finnish Trust Fund, a consultancy will assess options to accelerate provision of rural communications services in Cambodia.	Active
Dominican Republic	TA to design the "Fondo para el Desarrollo de las Telecomunicaciones (FDT)", created by law, to provide financial incentives to expand telecommunication services to rural and other underserved areas, including telephones, telecenters, distance learning and telehealth services. TA includes demographic and demand studies; a strategic plan and specific guidelines with administrative, fiscal, financial, and legal aspects of the FDT; and a program to implement the FDT.	Active
Ecuador	TA to create a rural telecommunications development fund, possibly together with energy, design its procedures and regulations, train personnel and provide guidance in the initial bidding phase. The fund will finance telecenters as well as rural telephony. A small initial investment into the fund is also foreseen.	Under preparation
Ghana	InfoDev grant to develop a business plan for the establishment and operation of a network of for-profit, information service centers in Ghana to be located in currently unserved communities.	Active
Guatemala	TA to prepare procedures and regulations and support subsidy auctions of the "Fondo de desarrollo de las telecomunicaciones (Fondetel)", created by law, and funded by 70 percent of revenues obtained from spectrum auctions.	Completed
Guatemala	E-government component in new public sector financial management project will support the creation of a portal for municipal governments and provide publicly accessible Internet-enabled terminals in some 50 municipalities.	Under preparation
India	Study to assess options to expand the reach of telecommunications services to the rural areas and the urban poor.	Active
Indonesia	Options study to identify three different economically viable schemes for providing rural telecommunications, with particular emphasis in the technology, including pilots. Potential TA to follow to assess the creation of a rural telecommunications fund.	Active
Kenya	InfoDev grant. Field trial of several rural telecommunications systems, and formulation of key policy elements for the rural telecommunications market, such as the establishment of private sector operating licenses or franchises for the provision of rural telephone service.	Completed
Madagascar	TA to develop a strategy to improve access to telecommunications and information services for rural and disadvantaged communities. TA will also develop tender documents for first round of bidding of a rural access fund. The project could finance the subsidy portion associated with selected region.	Active
Mali	TA to develop a strategy to improve the connectivity of rural localities using smart subsidy schemes.	Under preparation
Mauritania	TA to assist the Government in developing a strategy to pilot the	Active

	improvement of access to information delivery services for rural and disadvantaged communities. TA includes a rural strategy study, a postal development plan and a National Workshop	
Morocco	TA to assess options to expand rural coverage primarily with private investment. The study is open to the potential use of a fund with a competitive bidding scheme if fully commercial operation is deemed not viable in certain areas.	Completed
Mozambique	TA to develop a strategy to improve rural access to ICTs. TA will also develop tender documents for first round of bidding of a pilot fund, to be created through the project. The subsidy portion of this first round will be partially financed through the project.	Under preparation
Nepal	TA to create rural development fund and initial investment into the fund. Strategy is to introduce competition by licensing 4 new providers in separate regions with a rural focus. The project will finance the subsidy portion associated with one region initially.	Active
Nicaragua	TA to create telecommunications development fund to improve access to telecommunications and information services in rural and underserved areas. TA includes legal creation of the fund, demand studies, regulations and guidelines and bidding documents for first round of bidding. A small investment into the fund is also foreseen, which will also finance telecenters.	Active
Niger	TA to develop a strategy to improve access to telecommunications and information services for rural and disadvantaged communities and organization of an international workshop to adopt an implementation plan and coordinate donor activity in Niger for rural communications projects.	Active
Nigeria	TA to develop a strategy to improve access to telecommunications and information services for rural and disadvantaged communities. TA will also develop tender documents for first round of bidding of a pilot fund, to be created through the project. Also included in the project is a small investment into this pilot fund to conduct first phase of bidding.	Active
Philippines	The Public-Private Infrastructure Advisory Facility is funding a consultancy to provide advisory services to the Philippine Department of Transport and Communications regarding options to improve communications services in rural areas, possibly involving the creation of a universal access fund.	Active
Poland	Vast rural development program that includes rural telecommunications as part of a large infrastructure component. Potentially financing both studies and infrastructure.	Active
Senegal	TA to develop a strategy to improve the connectivity of rural localities using smart subsidy schemes.	Under preparation
South Africa	IDF grant to finance TA to prepare a report and action plan for the Ministry of Communications on ways of achieving universal access, including entrepreneurial alternatives for rural telecommunications.	Completed
Tanzania	TA to support a small working group under the leadership of the Minister's Telecommunications Policy Advisor to further develop a national strategy for rural telecommunications.	Under preparation
Togo	TA to assess options to develop rural telecommunications, establish licensing and interconnection regime to support rural operators, and select a few sites to conduct pilots.	Active
Uganda	Rural electrification project with ICT component aimed at creating a number of rural telecenters.	Active
African region	Two InfoDev grants: (1) regulatory models for satellite services in Africa, (2) universal access regulatory harmonization across Africa.	Active

In addition to the above mentioned projects, which explicitly support measures to improve access, most of the privatization projects in the telecommunications portfolio have implicitly dealt with improving access under the "traditional" approach of imposing service obligations to the privatized operator, particularly when coupled with some period of exclusivity. This is not the Bank's preferred approach, but given particular circumstances in some countries that are not conducive to the introduction of competition from day one, it is likely that in most cases there will remain a combination of implicit and explicit support mechanisms.

5.2   IFC Experience

IFC's telecommunications portfolio has also undergone dramatic changes in the past decade, shifting from major investments in privatized fixed networks to a larger amount of smaller investments in cellular operations. A number of operations are also explicitly targeted at bridging the access gap.

For instance, in 1997 IFC made a small investment in Datel Tanzania Limited, to provide data transmission and Internet access to remote businesses, government organizations, and schools in Tanzania, including in rural areas. In mid-1999, IFC invested in Grameen Phone, the largest cellular phone operator in Bangladesh, which will not only help expand its nationwide cellular telecommunications network, but will also provide the opportunity to expand is franchise network of community telephones to 30,000 villages in rural Bangladesh[32].

In addition, IFC has invested in a number of cellular ventures with rural or universal access obligations, such as Rwandacell, a national cellular operator in Rwanda, Mobile Systems International Cellular Investments Holdings (MSICIH), a holding company with multiple cellular operating networks in Africa or MobilRom, Romania's second cellular operator, among others.

On the other hand, IFC's investments in fixed-line operators have included in certain occasions specific provisions to improve community access, such as in Venezuela, where IFC's investment in CANTV foresees a component to build about 130 telecenters.

5.3   Emerging Lessons from World Bank Group Operations

While it is too soon to extract lessons learned from these nascent projects, some trends are appearing in these operations:

- With few exceptions, the focus of these projects is primarily on basic telephony, although a few projects do have the objective of promoting access to Internet services, as well as some that involve the postal sector;

- Bank operations in the LAC region are pioneering the implementation of telecommunications development funds, closely following the success of the Chile and Peru models;

- In other regions operations tend to be more cautious, starting with an options study to develop a rural/universal access strategy, although the trend towards universal access funds is gaining momentum;

---

[32] As mentioned above, see Cina Lawson and Natalie Meyenn, *Bringing Cellular Phone Service to Rural Areas*, World Bank Viewpoint Note No. 205, March 2000.

- The use of Bank/IDA investment as seed money into these newly created funds is still perceived as an experiment, although there is increasing interest and the portfolio is growing rapidly.

- IT components of Bank operations still tend to have their primary focus on macroeconomic reform (supporting tax and customs modernization, among others) . However, a few new projects are supporting the poverty reduction agenda through modernization and computerization of municipal governments and the provision of e-government services;

- Bank operations in support to content creation for and by the poor, be it through traditional or new media, remain nonexistent, despite the findings included in the 1999 WDR[33], which highlights the important role of the media in providing access to relevant and usable knowledge for the poor;

- IFC participation in rural/universal access projects is limited primarily to cellular operations. However, the scope may widen in the short to medium term with the consolidation of the new class of rural telecommunications operators, which would benefit of partnering with IFC in order to enter in riskier environments, such as in Sub-Saharan Africa;

- InfoDev is at the cutting edge of the Bank's activities in this area as in many others, allowing for innovation and experimentation along two major axes: with new technologies that may prove better adapted to the provision of services to sparsely populated areas, and with new regulatory models that may be more suited to low-income countries ;

Given this diversity of experiences, it is necessary to develop a strategic approach for current and future Bank Group rural/universal access operations. The final section of this paper is an attempt at cataloguing and classifying these operations, within the context of the new Bank-wide ICT Sector Strategy Paper.

---

[33] World Bank, "Knowledge for Development" 1998/99 World Development Report.

6 TOWARD A STRATEGY FOR UNIVERSAL ACCESS

6.1 Objectives

Building on the initial steps just outlined, the World Bank Group now needs to move towards a more proactive and concerted approach to addressing issues of access to information and communications and their linkages with poverty. Low degrees of rural access, and sharp urban-rural disparities, are defining characteristics of the global digital divide, increasingly of concern to both developing and developed countries, and therefore to international development agencies.

The World Bank can achieve the greatest value-added by addressing the problem of rural access as a fundamental step in closing the digital divide. An optimum mix of policies and investments is needed to expand the telecommunications network and close the access gap. The following four strategic directions are suggested as key areas of Bank activity to achieve this objective. These four strategic directions, which are not mutually exclusive, nor without a fair degree of overlap, are the following:

- Design and implement the most **appropriate policies and regulatory instruments** to promote universal access, addressing both the market efficiency gap and the access gap.
- Mobilize financing for **investments** and transactions in communications networks and companies, especially in those with the greatest development impact.
- Build **institutions and human capacity** in borrowers to adapt, implement and make best use of ICTs.
- **Pilot new approaches, create and disseminate knowledge**, and raise awareness within the WBG and with borrowers, partners, and the public.

Interventions along these four directions can have a profound impact in achieving the goals stated across Country Assistance Strategies (CAS), as summarily expressed in the following table. This table only intends to depict the primary linkages between the four strategic directions and some of the most recurrent CAS goals.

Table 6.1. Universal access and CAS goals

Key CAS objective	Impact of strategic direction			
	Policy Reform	Mobilization of Investment	Institutional Development	Pilot Projects and Knowledge
Improve macroeconomic stability and attract FDI	✔	✔	✔	
Improve governance and build institutions			✔	✔
Private sector led growth and competitiveness	✔	✔		
Integration into global economy	✔	✔		✔
Promoting human development			✔	✔
Decentralization and rural and social development	✔	✔	✔	✔

The sections below discuss these four strategic directions in greater detail. We first discuss the "what", i.e., policies and developmental activities included under each heading. We then explore the "how", that is, specific instruments that can be combined to reach the desired goals.

6.2 Strategic Directions

POLICY, LEGAL AND REGULATORY REFORM

The development of a stable, predictable and transparent policy, legal and regulatory framework is a prerequisite for any sustainable approach to improving access to information and communications services. Specific policy reform interventions can be structured along the three primary areas discussed below.

Addressing the 'market efficiency gap'

The guiding principle in introducing reforms addressed at bridging the market efficiency gap is the notion that access to communications is essential for the development of poor communities and therefore even poor rural and peri-urban communities are prepared to spend a portion of their incomes on communications. Based on this guiding principle, the preferred approach for any Bank intervention is to support policies that fully exploit the potential of the market in reaching out to these communities. In this respect, the three key principles of privatization, competition, and optimal regulation are the foundations of a policy regime that addresses the market efficiency gap.

Sound policies that promote the privatization of the incumbent monopoly, the introduction of competition in different segments of the sector, and promote pro-competitive regulation, and a regulatory environment that is conducive to a well-functioning, competitive and private sector-led market, are necessary to elicit investor confidence and create a level playing field. Bank assistance in this area includes support to the development of fair interconnection and revenue sharing arrangements; cost-oriented tariffs, and the elimination of internal cross-subsidies; fair, transparent and equitable access to scarce resources; as well as recourse to a strong and truly independent regulatory agency.

One particular market segment of the telecommunications industry which should be immediately liberalized, irrespective of other mechanisms, is the retail segment: pay phone, PCO, teleboutique and telecenter operators. In addition, immediate liberalization of value-added services, including Internet, as well as licensing new cellular operators, is an important step in improving access to services. It is also particularly important to give cellular operators the option in their licenses to provide fixed-wireless services within their cellular operating areas, which will allow them to serve rural areas at an incremental cost, rather than at full cost.

Addressing the 'access gap'

In the cases where there is doubt that relying on purely market-driven mechanisms may not bring access within the reach of all, the World Bank can support "universal access" policies aimed at narrowing the access gap, as described in the preceding chapters.

The starting point is to develop a universal access policy, that must define very precisely what service is targeted (although the default is public telephony), for what groups of people, who can provide it and how it is financed[34].

---

[34] For a comprehensive discussion of universal service policies, see Björn Wellenius, *Extending Telecommunications beyond the Market*, World Bank Viewpoint Note No. 206, March 2000.

A **universal access policy** can be developed with the support of an options study, which will evaluate different alternatives for increasing access to telecommunications and information services by the poor, particularly in rural and isolated areas. Based on an overall survey of the country situation, the study would develop in sufficient detail the available and recommended options, including the suggested implementation strategy. In particular, the options study would assess the opportunity of creating a universal access fund, and the general design parameters on which such fund would be based, including areas identified as priority targets for the implementation of the strategy.

A number of **regulatory interventions to implement a universal access fund** will have to be put into place, if the policy calls for the creation of such a fund. For instance, a legal reform may be needed to create the fund by law and give it the necessary financial autonomy, followed by a thorough demand study of priority regions. In addition, it will be necessary to develop regulatory instruments, such as fund regulations, cost models, economic analysis models, operational guidelines, operator licenses, franchisee agreements, and bidding documents for the competitive process to award subsidies from the fund. Finally, some technical assistance may be required during the first round of bidding, to ensure proper implementation of the newly developed regulatory instruments.

Advanced ICTs

Regarding access to services other than basic telephony, such as Internet access, universal access policies in developed countries tend to be separate from basic universal access policies, with clearly distinct management, funding, and service provision mechanisms. While this approach is preferable, in some developing countries this separation is difficult, given the limited availability of funds and regulatory capacity, coupled with the perception that they are quickly staying behind in the area of Internet access. Chile, Peru, South Africa, and others have already included the provision of Internet access and telecenters in small towns as part of their universal access fund bidding processes. Using similar mechanisms to promote both the "old" and the "new" access agendas is acceptable as long as the new one is limited to very targeted interventions with minimal burden on the development of the sector and maximum developmental impact. Indeed, in the case of Chile, financial support for telecenters through the universal access fund happened only after it was clear that the fund was running a surplus.

In addition, for rapid development of the Internet, it is important to promote local call access over a wide area (not just in major cities), as well as technology freedom, including the use of radio spectrum by ISPs wanting to extend reliable and faster speed service to rural areas and to telecenters. The market for leased lines and international connectivity plays a key role in the diffusion of the Internet to minor towns and rural areas: the more liberalized and competitive it is, the more affordable the prices for Internet access will be throughout the country.

MOBILIZATION OF INVESTMENT

Ensuring sustainability and quality of service provision in an environment of limited public funds and management capacity requires relying primarily on the private sector to make the necessary investments to build and extend the basic infrastructure. World Bank Group investments in rural telecommunications and telecenter operators will therefore be led primarily by IFC and MIGA. However, in a number of cases, there is scope for World Bank investments, as described below.

Investments in telecommunications operators

The leadership role of IFC and MIGA in this area will be critical in providing financing, mitigating investor risk, and leveraging private sector investment in rural and underserved markets. Indeed, we noted above the fact that recent regulatory reforms have attracted new telecommunications operators into the rural access market, and that these operators have taken risks to develop this new sector. Some have demonstrated that, with a well-defined business plan, there are commercially viable opportunities they find worth developing. However, access to risk mitigation measures would definitely enhance the development potential of these new players, encouraging their entry in environments perceived more commercially and/or politically risky.

Seed financing of universal access funds

In some cases, however, it may be necessary to leverage private investment with some minimal public contribution. This would entail the creation of some kind of time bound "universal access" support mechanism to extend service to areas, which would have remained unserved if left to the market forces alone. The preferred support mechanisms will be of an explicit nature, such as the creation of a fund, rather than implicit mechanisms, such as cross-subsidies and/or interconnection surcharges. In addition, the allocation of subsidies should be done competitively, in an open and transparent bidding process, as was explained above for the cases of Chile and Peru, among others.

The primary universal access support mechanism is therefore a fund, aimed at providing targeted one-time subsidies for initial investment in service expansion, so as to stretch the limits of the market without unduly distorting it. This fund, managed by the independent regulator or another independent third party, would be financed through contributions from all players in the sector of about 1 percent of their annual turnover. Direct subsidies from the public budget should be avoided in general, since public funds are scarce and could be at risk of being available only on an irregular basis or discontinued altogether.

However, in low-income economies, with very underdeveloped telecommunications sectors, such a small contribution to the fund may mean very low revenues for the fund in its initial stages, which may require a substantial initial injection of public monies into the fund. This is justified as a way of accelerating the achievement of a critical mass of funds to make an impact. This initial "jump-starting" of the fund, particularly in IDA countries, can be financed with a World Bank investment, if overall progress in reforming the sector is considered satisfactory. This World Bank investment can be structured as a component of a loan or credit, to cover the initial government contribution to the fund, provided the fund regulations meet with the acceptance of the World Bank. Such public contribution can itself be structured as a loan from the government to the fund against future revenues of the fund, or, more frequently, as a one-time exceptional government subsidy.

Advanced ICTs and SMEs

The World Bank Group can play an important role in supporting the establishment of telecenters, coupled with tele-learning and tele-health initiatives, as well as promoting the effective adoption of ICTs by small- and medium-sized enterprises. This will not only build increased revenue potential on rural operator networks, thus facilitating sustainability of their service, but will also give local residents public access to information services and support the development of the private sector.

Support to telecenters can be implemented through universal access mechanisms similar to those described above. This approach has recently been experimented in Chile and Peru, and the first network of telecenters financed through the universal access funds is currently being installed in both countries. However, this is still at an experimental phase, and the economic analysis tools used to analyze rural pay phone projects are still in the process of being carefully adapted and fine-tuned so that they can be applicable to telecenters.

An alternative approach is to set up a national or regional program of matching grants and micro-loans, or a venture capital fund for Internet start-ups. These financing mechanisms can be considered as a means to encourage and foster the emergence of an entrepreneurial cadre of community leaders, incubators and small business people in the tele-business and high-tech fields. Such a cadre is already growing in many places, in the form of local 'telephone shop' operators, which can be easily scaled up to small telecenters, rather than focusing on larger 'top down' institution-oriented telecenters. These projects could, for example, finance the purchase of a single PC, software, scanner and modem; or a small network, router and initial Internet access costs. They could also support Internet service providers to put in new access nodes outside the main cities, or 'soft' investments such as web site or content creation.

These investments can also be considered to be a means of fostering the development of the private sector and local enterprises in general, by supporting the uptake of modern ICTs in less favored regions or where a specific industry is of strategic importance for the country given its weight in the overall economy. Where sector-specific nongovernmental organizations or industry organizations exist, which substantially represent the interests of a particular industry, these organizations may be the most effective way of channeling grants or micro-loans for the effective use of ICTs aimed at improving the productivity of those industries, by allowing small enterprises access to a PC and an e-mail or Internet connection to communicate among themselves.

INSTITUTIONAL DEVELOPMENT

In order for public policies to have a chance at reaching their objectives, it is often important to enhance the capacity of the institutions in charge of their implementation. The following paragraphs explore two specific cases of particular relevance for universal access policies.

Regulatory agencies

The establishment of well-functioning institutions to manage the policy and regulatory process is one of the priorities in reforming the telecommunications sector. A key institution which consistently requires strengthening in most, if not all, telecommunications sector reform programs is an independent regulator, capable of establishing and enforcing the rules of fair competition in an open market, without interferences. World Bank support in this area is directed at legal reforms that will guarantee both operational and financial autonomy for these regulators, as a way of securing their independence.

This is even more critical in the cases where the regulator is at the same time in charge of implementing universal access policies and programs, in particular, through direct management of a universal access fund. Managing such a fund with true independence, transparency and efficiency places an added burden on these nascent regulators, who need to secure the necessary human, material and financial resources. It becomes therefore critical, in order for these institutions to be both effective and efficient, that they be capable of attracting and retaining qualified staff and that they have access to the necessary tools to effectively conduct their tasks.

This requires a strong initial investment in organizational planning, personnel development and information systems, as well as for training and upgrading skills to allow staff to keep up with the constant evolution of the sector.

In the area of organizational planning, among other things, there would be a need to redesign the business processes and design the optimum organization to deal with universal access policies, be it as a unit within the regulator, or as a separate agency, as in the case of South Africa. If a fund is created, the entity tasked with administering it would have to be guaranteed the necessary independence with respect to sector players. In the case of a unit within the regulator, it must have a direct reporting line to the head of the regulatory agency. In addition, its financial integrity and accountability has to be ensured, through clear and transparent accounting, reporting and auditing mechanisms and a strict separation of accounts. Furthermore, it is very important to monitor the performance of this entity, to ensure the overhead in managing the fund as compared to the overall mass of funds administered, lies within a defined benchmark, typically less than 10 percent, and in many cases even as low as 1 percent.

Regarding training and outreach, Bank-financed universal access support operations must include training for policy-makers and regulators on the design and implementation of this type of programs. In addition, it is important that they are able to participate in international seminars and conferences where these issues are openly discussed, to ensure they learn about similar initiatives elsewhere and keep abreast with new developments in this area.

E-government

The World Bank is also playing an important role, through ICT components of public sector management projects, in supporting the modernization of government agencies, notably those which play an active role in poverty reduction and rural development, such as planning, census, social security, and land administration agencies, as well as provincial and municipal governments, in addition to rural and peri-urban schools and health centers, among others.

Given the lack of relevant content for local communities currently available over the Internet, a critical strategy for bridging the digital divide is to encourage adoption by government, notably by municipal governments, of modern information technology and provision of services over the Internet, accessible from within community telecenters.

Support for such a strategy can be provided by means of matching grants or micro-loans, coupled with seminars, computer and Internet literacy programs, or other measures aimed at raising awareness about new technologies at the community level.

However, the best approach to modernizing the public sector is by effective use of public-private partnerships. Outsourcing of ICT services, may be an effective way of modernizing the public sector without excessively burdening the government budget and at the same time promoting the emergence of a thriving high-tech private sector. In particular, the web-hosting or application service provider model can be very useful in providing a common set of tools to a large pool of customers (e.g., municipal governments).

Initiatives aimed at improving access to communications may become moot if the content provided is not relevant for the intended recipient. The 1999 World Development Report highlighted that one of the most powerful tools in fighting against poverty is the provision of relevant knowledge to the poor, in a manner they can use. This implies the existence of the appropriate channels for two-way communication: from poor communities to the rest of the world and vice versa. Governments must therefore put emphasis in creating local knowledge, "giving the poor voice" and learning about the poor from the poor, adopting existing "international" knowledge and adapting it to the local conditions.

Pilot projects

One of the primary forms of knowledge creation and dissemination the Bank Group should continue to be engaged in is pilot projects, which allow for experimentation with new mechanisms for addressing the access gap, through policy and regulatory arrangements, new financing schemes, and using cutting edge technologies. It is in this area where the Bank and IFC can obtain the maximum leverage from infoDev's activities, for instance, which allow for small scale "test-driving" of new concepts in a controlled environment, before large scale implementation can take place, creating vast amounts of knowledge in the process. However, it is important to build independent assessment tools into the design of pilot projects, to allow for proper evaluation of their financial sustainability and impact that will guarantee successful up-scaling.

These pilot projects have proven to be very effective in raising awareness worldwide of the need to bring access to information and communications services within the reach of the poor. They have also led to the creation of a distributed human network and community of practice, with members from both the private and the public sector, which IFC and the Bank find useful to tap, in their efforts to replicate and scale-up these initial "experiments". Examples are small-scale ICT diffusion programs among SMEs or among local organizations, using grants or micro-loans, and seminars, conferences or itinerant expositions dedicated to raising awareness about new technologies, computer literacy programs in schools and community centers, and experiments such as the "hole in the wall" project[35].

Pilot projects also allow to experiment with innovative ways of combining several types of communications tools so as to reach more people. Examples of this could be using the post office as a natural access point for e-mail and other Internet services for rural and peri-urban populations. Similarly, the Internet can be very effectively combined with radio broadcasting at the community level, e.g., through community organizations with access to the Internet, that develop and broadcast radio programs with information found on the Web, which is adapted to local needs.

Knowledge about the poor

Poverty reduction requires a clear understanding of the needs, priorities, demands, and

---

[35] This experiment consisted in installing an Internet-enabled terminal in the wall of a research center in India and allowing the local slum population, primarily children, use it without any specific guidance. Within days, the children, with little knowledge of English, were able to effectively use the computer and browse the Internet, locating content of interest to them, such as popular hindi songs.

pressures of the poor. Household and community surveys, such as the LSMS surveys[36], and demand studies, based on different socioeconomic parameters, including spending patterns on communications, are an important means of gaining this knowledge. This is a first step in developing participatory universal access programs, which involve local communities in the design of such development projects through demand assessments and by allowing them to participate in the decisions about the location of particular information access outlets.

Locally relevant content

Creation of locally relevant content would entail the development and/or adaptation to local conditions and language of existing information relevant to the needs of poor communities, such as school curricula, health, or agricultural information. A combination of these with radio dissemination tools is the most effective way of reaching isolated or otherwise disadvantaged communities.

Additional sources of relevant local content would be websites with on-line news and local government information, as mentioned above. The Bank can support the development of websites in local languages, especially when combined with initiatives to promote telecenters and other forms of public access to information (such as through schools, or health centers) in rural areas and poor neighborhoods. By establishing and promoting the use of local telecenters and infoshops[37], which may be coupled with local businesses, schools and/or health centers, simple e-commerce solutions can also be provided to local communities to establish their own marketing and sales channels for local products. The Bank is already supporting programs such as "PeopLink"[38], which allows artisans in the developing world to sell their products on-line to customers in developed countries.

Knowledge sharing

Coupled with the support to institutional development of regulatory agencies, conferences at the national or regional level can be organized to openly discuss issues related to universal access with all stakeholders, including the investor community. This can be an important step in securing consensus toward the need for a universal access fund or other support mechanism, as well as a vehicle to exchange ideas, assessments of pilot projects, and stories of success and/or failure.

SUMMARY OF PROPOSED STRATEGIC DIRECTIONS

The following tables summarize and classify the above policies and investment alternatives described based, respectively, on the different strategic areas identified and the country groups established in the previous chapters.

---

[36] See http://www.worldbank.org/lsms/
[37] In most cases, since Internet access is probably one of the priorities of these centers, it may be a good idea to make sure they are equipped with automatic translation tools and even voice-enabled interfaces for the illiterate.
[38] See http://www.peoplink.org/

Table 6.2. Policies supported by strategic direction

Strategic Directions	Policy / investment options
Policy reform	• Competition, regulation, privatization • Universal access funds, including for advanced ICTs
Mobilization of investment	• Investment in rural and telecenter operators • Seed financing of universal access funds • Grants and micro-loans for SME development
Institutional development	• Organizational planning and capacity building for regulatory agencies • Modernization of government agencies and local administrations, and e-government initiatives
Pilot projects and knowledge	• Pilots to innovate policy and technology for universal access, including proper independent assessment • Household surveys and participatory approach to policy development and implementation • Local content creation and dissemination

Table 6.3. Activities supported by country group[39]

Liberalization/ Challenge rating	Monopoly	Only mobile competition	Partially liberal	Open market
GROUP 1 Remote and challenging areas, high economic disparity	Introduce competition (at least in Internet, mobile, pay phones) Privatize incumbent Create regulatory institutions and build capacity	Continue liberalization Institutional development of regulator Create Universal Access Fund,	Fully liberalize market Institutional development of regulator Invest in rural and telecenter operators Create Universal Access Fund, possibly with seed finance	Institutional development of regulator Invest in rural and telecenter operators Create Universal Access Fund, possibly with seed finance
GROUP 2 Significant variations	Same as above	Same as above	Same as above, but may not require seed finance	Same as above but focus of fund equally on advanced ICTs
GROUP 3 Uniform and/or small country	Same as above	Same as above, except fund is not required	Same as above, except fund is not required	Same as above, but primary focus of fund on advanced ICTs

---

[39] Note that the activities under the third and fourth strategic directions are applicable to all country groups, and are therefore omitted from the table for simplicity.

6.3   Implementation and Monitoring

The following sections discuss how the strategic areas outlined above could be implemented. The first section discusses the World Bank Group instruments that can be used, the subsequent section discusses the different stages of implementation, starting with piloting the strategy in selected countries, building consensus and partnerships and monitoring and evaluation.

WORLD BANK GROUP INSTRUMENTS

World Bank Group instruments can be combined in different ways to provide optimal support to governments embarking in pro-poor reforms of the ICT sector. In most cases of IBRD/IDA financing, a universal access support operation will be a component of a larger project, in some cases multi-sectoral, so choice of instrument will have to be done in conjunction with the other components. The following table shows which instruments appear most appropriate for specific kinds of intervention. Possible concrete operations are shown vertically in the table, and their potential primary components horizontally. The combination of both would constitute a final product, which is shown in the table as a tick.

Table 6.4. World Bank Group instruments in support of the strategic directions identified

	IBRD/IDA*						InfoDev**	IFC***	MIGA‡
	TAL	LIL	SIL	Guar.	(P)SAL & Others†	WBI			
Policy and regulatory reform	✔	✔			✔		✔		
Investment financing^	✔	✔	✔	✔				✔	✔
Institution building	✔	✔			✔	✔	✔	✔	
Pilot projects and knowledge	✔	✔				✔	✔	✔	✔

*   IBRD/IDA instruments include: TAL is Technical Assistance Loan (or Credit); LIL is Learning and Innovation Loan (or Credit); SIL for Sectoral Investment Loan (or Credit); Guar. for Bank guarantees; (P)SAL for (Programmatic) Structural Adjustment Loan (or Credit); WBI for World Bank Institute, the training and outreach arm of the Bank.

**   infoDev is a Bank-administered multilateral grant program to promote the use of information technologies for development. See http://www.infodev.org.

***   IFC has a range of loan, equity, and guarantee financial instruments. It also provides financial advisory services.

‡   MIGA guarantees cover risks of transfer restriction, expropriation, breach of contract, war and civil disturbance for qualified investments in developing member countries.

†   Other possible instruments may include SECAL and APL, as well as ESW, albeit limited to policy dialogue.

^   World Bank Group financing to come in the first instance from IFC and MIGA. IBRD/IDA as a financier of last resort in the context of an appropriately dimensioned partnership between the public and private sectors in higher risk environments.

Both Technical Assistance Loans (TALs) and LILs appear to be the most appropriate vehicle to package elements from all four strategic areas into one single operation. In the case of LILs, given their small size, these operations could be stand-alone. However, it seems that the use of LILs as theoretically innovative and fast instruments may have been hindered in practice by excessively bureaucratic and long preparation periods, prompting the need for a critical assessment of their appropriateness on a case-by-case basis.

TALs will continue to be the primary instruments for delivery of IBRD/IDA support, notably in the area of policy and regulatory reform, through the design of a universal access strategy and implementation of required legal and regulatory reforms, as discussed above.

Regarding investments, while it has been explicit Bank policy since 1995 not to use IBRD/IDA funds to finance infrastructure investments in the telecommunications sector, there is scope for small exceptions that are not harmful to competition. We are referring to the examples given above of Nepal, Nicaragua, and others, where due to the extra effort required to entice private investment in rural and poor areas, Bank seed finance is foreseen for the universal access fund. In addition to "jump-starting" the fund, an initial Bank-financed public investment into the fund would make it possible to obtain early results, thus having an important demonstrative effect, as well as providing a means of securing widespread consensus from sector players toward the implementation of this novel policy. Annex 5 elaborates more on how to select countries for this type of investment and how to estimate the appropriate level of Bank funding.

IFC can play an important role in enhancing the success of Bank universal access fund bidding processes, if the possibility of a downstream IFC investment in the winning bidder is clearly perceived by the potential investors, such as through explicit mention in the bidding documents.

When the size of the investment is too small to justify other instruments, TALs, although not intended for this purpose, may continue to be used, particularly if packaged with regulatory reform. This can be implemented as an investment component in a Bank loan/credit to finance in part, a number of universal access projects, selected in accordance with the fund guidelines and involving not only public telephony, but possibly also telecenters. IBRD/IDA financing would cover the one-time government contribution to the fund, disbursable against the selection of the winning bidder in accordance with international competitive bidding procedures[40].

When large investments are foreseen, compared to the amount of technical assistance involved, **Sector Investment Loans (SILs)** may be a more appropriate mechanism to provide this seed financing to the universal access fund. Such an instrument may also be the preferred mechanism to implement the grant and/or micro-loan programs mentioned above for the purposes of improving use of ICTs by SMEs. In addition, the recently established joint Bank/IFC SME Capacity Building Facility, which has as one of its strategic pillars improving access to information and technology for SMEs, can be a very valuable resource.

In the area of institutional development and capacity building, TALs will also continue to be the primary vehicle to provide assistance to regulators in implementing universal access policies. This can take the shape of support to the creation of the appropriate organizational structure, and long-term advisory services by experienced international consultants, as well as in the training and participation in regulatory events.

---

[40] In this context, a specific provision in the Bank's procurement guidelines (3.13 a) can constitute an appropriate vehicle for actual implementation of such a component.

In the area of training, however, the **World Bank Institute** can continue to play an important role, through the development and delivery of international training seminars and conferences on different aspects of industry regulation, facilitating transborder learning and sharing of experiences. Similarly, **infoDev** grants can support participation of developing country officials to international seminars and conferences, through such specific programs as the various scholarship funds.

However, **the bulk of WBG investments should come from IFC and MIGA** instruments. As the Bank seeks to support policy reform and the establishment of universal access funds in various countries, IFC can play a crucial role in partnering with seasoned players in order to increase their capacity to commit resources and shoulder what their investors often perceive as heavier market risk.

IFC investments in mobile operators and pre-privatization investments in fixed-line operators have implicitly made an impact in provision of services to rural and underserved areas. However, a more explicit approach could entail IFC and MIGA operations that target low-income areas. In the case of IFC, this could take the form of **debt and/or equity investments** in some of the new players that have sprung up as a result of the recent universal access fund bidding processes in Latin America, to help them scale-up and invest in other regions. An example of such a partnership between an international finance institution and a rural telecommunications operator already exists: the Inter-American Development Bank approved in 1999, a $25 million loan to CTR under Chile's Rural Telecommunications Development Fund.

MIGA, on the other hand, can provide **investment guarantees** against non-commercial risk, particularly in countries where perceived political risk may be high. MIGA's IPAnet website, aimed at providing a one-stop shopping experience to investors seeking specific investment opportunities in developing countries, is an excellent vehicle for dissemination of such opportunities in the sector. The site, although not specifically targeting investments in rural and poor areas, does give access to important legal, regulatory and financial information, which could be easily enhanced with specific sections on opportunities for investment in rural telephony, and telecenter operators, among others.

Some of these operators, their parent companies, and new players including African based cellular operators with years of experience, are now interested in moving into Africa's rural market. However, Africa, where the perceived risk is higher, but so are the potential returns, stands to win most from support by IFC and/or MIGA.

IFC-financed venture funds and micro-finance operations can be envisaged to promote investments in rural or peri-urban phone shops and telecenters, as well as Internet ventures, such as incubators or Application Service Providers, particularly targeting SMEs and local administrations. Direct support to SMEs can be provided through the SME Capacity Building Facility mentioned above.

IFC's advisory services and technical assistance programs can play an important role in supporting institutional development and capacity building. Technical assistance can be provided to private operators interested in entering the rural market. Advisory services can be provided to the public sector, e.g. acting as an investment bank in the selection of winning bidders in universal access fund subsidy auctions.

Pilot country selection

In order to generate consensus toward the strategy, we propose that a small number of "pilot countries" be selected, which can allow us to demonstrate how the wide range of Bank Group instruments can be used effectively in the implementation of the most appropriate mix of universal access policies and financing instruments.

We have used the table of country categories introduced in chapter four, which is reproduced below, where the proposed countries are shown in bold. The criteria that have been used in selecting these countries are the following:

- that the Bank currently has ongoing or is preparing operations in the selected countries, in which universal access is an explicit goal ,
- that the IFC is or could be interested in operations in the selected countries,
- that the sample has wide geographic representation, with countries from all regions, if possible,
- that the sample represents countries that fall within the different categories in accordance with their liberalization stage and "challenge" rating,
- that the sample includes at least one country that would require Bank/IDA seed financing as was explained above.

Table 6.5. Pilot country selection.

Liberalization/ Challenge rating	Monopoly	Only mobile competition	Partially liberal	Open market
GROUP 3 Remote areas and/or high economic disparity	**Nepal ▶**	Burkina Faso Chad Kenya ▶ **Mozambique** Niger Senegal South Africa	Angola **Bolivia ▶** **Brazil ▶** China Indonesia Mali Mauritania **Nigeria ▶** Russia Tanzania Venezuela ▶	Argentina Australia Canada Chile Colombia Madagascar Mexico Peru U.S.
GROUP 2 Significant variations	Gambia **Nicaragua ▶**	Botswana Bulgaria Cote d'Ivoire Ecuador ▶ Jordan **Morocco ▶** Romania	Ghana Honduras India ▶ Kyrgyz Rep. Sri Lanka Thailand	**Dominican Rep.** Finland Guatemala Malaysia Philippines **Uganda**
GROUP 1 Uniform, densely populated and/or small country		Gabon Greece Hungary ▶ ▶ Latvia Malawi Slovak Rep.	Bangladesh Poland ▶ Togo	El Salvador **Georgia** New Zealand UK

Strategy implementation and evaluation

In order to implement this strategy in a specific country context, one would first have to identify the most appropriate mix of policies and financing schemes, as well as instruments to support these. It would involve the following activities:

- understanding the specific conditions of the country, identifying what country group it would fall under (as described above), and what the policy implications would be;
- understanding the degree of its market efficiency gap, which, if large, would attest to the need for a liberalized policy and regulatory environment to bridge this gap;
- identifing the size of the true 'access gap', arising from its geoeconomic challenge, and select policies and financing strategies to bridge it, including, if necessary, the use of competitively bid subsidies;
- selecting the appropriate impact and monitoring indicators;
- if the selected policy option is to use a fund, a decision also has to be made regarding the potential role for Bank seed financing, and the amount of such financing. A proposed approach is described in Annex 5.

Evaluation of the impact of a specific operation can be done by monitoring a number of impact indicators. Examples could include the following[41]:

- Access to service in rural areas or among the poorest: telephone/Internet density in rural areas; percentage of poor households/SMEs with a private line, PC, access to Internet; number of locations with at least one pay phone or telecenter;

- Cost and quality of service: number of complaints; various user tariffs; expenditure per household/SME (as a percentage of revenue);

- Operator performance: number of lines/telecenters installed; amount of money invested; subsidy received, if any, per line/telecenter installed or as a percentage of investment; profitability indicators;

- Institutional performance: number of man-hours of training delivered; effectiveness and efficiency of subsidy/grant management (number and size of subsidies/grants provided, overhead as a percentage of program funds allocated, etc.); amounts invested in ICTs (also in percentage of institutional budget);

- Content indicators: investments in application and content development; number of web pages developed; percentage of web pages in local language.

Many of the above indicators can be measured both at the aggregate (national) level or at the disaggregated or local level. In both cases it is important to correlate these with poverty-related indicators, such as income levels, access to other services, such as water, electricity, transportation, health, and education, etc, as well as quality of these services.

Measuring impact at the aggregate level can be done by recording the values of these indicators at the start of the program and monitoring their variation annually. In the case of a

---

[41] See other indicators in the ICT chapter of the PRSP Sourcebook:
http://www.worldbank.org/poverty/strategies/sourctoc.htm.

disaggregated analysis of the impact of the program, it is useful to record the values of the selected indicators in a set of locations not directly affected by the program, and monitor the differences between this control set and the locations directly targeted.

Overall, these monitoring indicators, updated annually and correlated with poverty indicators, will support the evaluation of the impact of the strategy in helping alleviate poverty, and allow for its fine-tuning in order to maximize the impact of the Bank Group's future operations.

ANNEXES

Most information in the following tables is based on ITU data and World Bank staff reports.

ANNEX 1: REGULATORY AND MARKET STRUCTURE OF SELECTED COUNTRIES

SUB-SAHARAN AFRICA	POLICY AND REGULATION			MARKET STRUCTURE		
	Pro-competitive Policy	New Telecoms Law	Independent Regulator	Cellular competition	Privatized incumbent	Competition in fixed services
Angola		✓	✓	✓		✓
Botswana	✓	✓	✓	✓		
Burkina Faso			✓	✓		
Chad		✓	✓			
Cote d'Ivoire	✓	✓	✓	✓	✓	
Gabon		✓	✓	✓		
Gambia						
Ghana	✓	✓	✓	✓	✓	✓[42]
Kenya	✓	✓	✓	✓[43]		✓[44]
Madagascar	✓	✓	✓	✓	✓	✓
Malawi	✓	✓	✓	✓		
Mali	✓	✓	✓	✓		
Mauritania	✓	✓	✓	✓	✓	✓
Mozambique	✓	✓	✓	✓		
Niger	✓	✓		✓	✓	✓[45]
Nigeria	✓	✓	✓	✓	✓	
Senegal	✓	✓	✓	✓	✓	
South Africa	✓	✓	✓	✓	✓	
Tanzania	✓	✓	✓	✓	✓	✓[46]
Togo	✓	✓	✓	✓		
Uganda	✓	✓	✓	✓	✓	✓

---

[42] Duopoly in international and national long distance (until 2002).
[43] Second cellular license issued in early 2000.
[44] 8 regional licenses were issued in 2000.
[45] Except for international service.
[46] Duopoly in the Zanzibar Island (TTCL and Zantel), in the mainland monopoly by TTCL.

LATIN AMERICA AND CARIBBEAN	POLICY AND REGULATION			MARKET STRUCTURE		
	Pro-competitive Policy	New Telecoms Law	Independent Regulator	Cellular competition	Privatized incumbent	Competition in fixed services
Argentina	✓	✓	✓	✓	✓	✓
Brazil	✓	✓	✓	✓	✓	✓[47]
Bolivia	✓	✓	✓	✓	✓	
Chile	✓	✓	✓	✓	✓	✓
Colombia	✓	✓	✓	✓		✓
Dominican Republic	✓	✓	✓	✓	✓	✓
Ecuador		✓	✓	✓[48]		
El Salvador	✓	✓	✓	✓	✓	✓
Guatemala	✓	✓	✓	✓	✓	✓
Honduras		✓	✓	✓		
Mexico	✓	✓	✓	✓	✓	✓
Nicaragua			✓	✓	✓	
Peru	✓	✓	✓	✓	✓	✓
Venezuela	✓	✓	✓	✓	✓	✓

---

[47] Duopoly: incumbent and "mirror" licensees.
[48] Two licensed mobile operators.

ASIA	POLICY AND REGULATION			MARKET STRUCTURE		
	Pro-competitive Policy	New Telecoms Law	Independent Regulator	Cellular competition	Privatized incumbent	Competition in fixed services
Bangladesh	✓	✓		✓		✓[49]
China	✓[50]			✓		✓
India	✓	✓	✓	✓	✓	✓[51]
Indonesia	✓	✓	✓	✓	✓	✓[52]
Malaysia	✓	✓	✓	✓	✓	✓
Nepal	✓	✓	✓	✓		✓[53]
Philippines	✓	✓	✓	✓	✓	✓
Sri Lanka	✓	✓	✓	✓	✓	✓[54]
Thailand	✓	✓	✓	✓		✓[55]

---

[49] Duopoly in local services.
[50] WTO offer.
[51] Except for international long distance.
[52] Duopoly in international long distance.
[53] Duopoly.
[54] Except for international long distance.
[55] Only local competition.

ECA[56] & MNA[57]	POLICY AND REGULATION			MARKET STRUCTURE		
	Pro-competitive Policy	New Telecoms Law	Independent Regulator	Cellular competition	Privatized incumbent	Competition in fixed services
Bulgaria	✓	✓	✓	✓		
Georgia	✓	✓	✓	✓	[58]	✓
Hungary	✓	✓	✓	✓	✓	
Kyrgyz Republic	✓	✓	✓	✓		✓[59]
Latvia	✓	✓		✓	✓	
Poland	✓	✓	✓	✓	✓	✓[60]
Romania	✓	✓		✓	✓	
Russian Fed.	✓	✓		✓	✓	✓[61]
Slovak Rep.		✓	✓	✓[62]	✓	
Jordan		✓	✓	✓[63]	✓	
Morocco	✓	✓	✓	✓[64]	✓	

ADVANCED COUNTRIES	POLICY AND REGULATION			MARKET STRUCTURE		
	Pro-competitive Policy	New Telecoms Law	Independent Regulator	Cellular competition	Privatized incumbent	Competition in fixed services
Australia	✓	✓	✓	✓	✓	✓
Canada	✓	✓	✓	✓	✓	✓
Finland	✓	✓	✓	✓	✓	✓
Greece	✓	✓	✓	✓	✓	✓
New Zealand	✓			✓	✓	✓
United Kingdom	✓	✓	✓	✓	✓	✓
United States	✓	✓	✓	✓	✓	✓

---

[56] Europe and Central Asia
[57] Middle East and North Africa
[58] Long distance incumbent partly privatized.
[59] Only local competition.
[60] All services liberalized, except international (will be liberalized by 2003).
[61] Duopoly.
[62] Duopoly.
[63] Duopoly.
[64] Duopoly.

REGION/Country (AFRICA)	US/UA def. Y	US/UA def. N	Focus Rural	Focus General	Incumbent	Cellular	Regional	Special rural license	Special pay phone operators	Phone shops & private PCOs	Telecenters	Innovative initiatives	Cross-subsidies	Interconnect fees	Fund N	Fund Y	Plan	Funded through	Carriers	Retailers	Subscribers
Angola	X			X	X	X							X			X		Operator levy	X		
Botswana	X		X		X	X							X		X						
Burkina Faso	X		X		X	X						X[65]			X						
Chad	X		X		X			X			X		X		X						
Côte d'Ivoire	X		X		X				X	X						X		Gov't, Op. levy	X		
Gabon		X			X								X		X						
Gambia		X			X[66]								X		X						
Ghana	X		X		X	X		X[67]		X	X		X				X	Op. levy	X		
Kenya	X		X	X	X	X	X[68]						X				X				
Madagascar	X		X		X								X		X						
Malawi	X		X		X	X							X				X				
Mali		X			X	X		X[69]			X		X		X				X		
Mauritania	X			X	X	X							X				X[70]				
Mozambique	X			X	X	X							X				X				
Niger	X			X	X	X					X		X		X						
Nigeria	X			X	X	X							X				X				
Senegal	X		X		X	X				X[71]	X		X		X						
South Africa	X			X	X	X				X	X		X			X		Op. levy	X	X[72]	X
Tanzania	X			X	X		X[73]				X[74]		X		X						
Togo	X		X		X					X[75]			X		X						
Uganda	X		X	X	X[76]	X				X	X		X			X		Op. levy	X		

---

[65] Virtual telephony
[66] Includes SNO obligations
[67] Capital Telecom provides WLL services in rural areas since 1997
[68] A number of local operators outside Nairobi were recently licensed
[69] Three rural telephony systems to cover around 60 villages are being financed by AFD [BMI 99]
[70] Created by law, to be implemented
[71] Privately owned and operated telecenters
[72] Primarily telecenters
[73] Zantel in Zanzibar Island
[74] PACT in co-operation with Acacia Initiative etc.
[75] A receive-only line managed by a private individual is available to the population of each locality to receive pre-arranged calls or messages
[76] Including SNO

Latin America

REGION/Country	US/UA def. Y	US/UA def. N	Focus: Rural	Focus: General	Incumbent	Cellular	Regional	Special rural license	Special pay phone operators	Phone shops & private PCOs	Telecenters	Innovative initiatives	Cross-subsidies	Interconnect fees	US/UA Fund N	US/UA Fund Y	US/UA Fund Plan	Funded through	Carriers	Retailers	Subscribers
LATIN AMERICA																					
Argentina	X			X	X	X				X	X		X				X	Pay or play	X		X
Bolivia	X		X		X		X[77]									X[78]		Gov't	X	X[81]	
Brazil	X		X		X[79]	X					X	X[80]				X		Operator levy	X		
Chile	X		X					X	X		X			X[82]		X		Gov't	X	X	
Colombia	X		X					X	X							X		Operator levy,[83] license fees	X		
Dominican Republic	X			X				X	X		X					X		Operator levy	X	X[84]	
Ecuador		X			X						X						X	Operator levy	X		
El Salvador		X									X[85]				X						
Guatemala	X		X		X[86]			X	X	X			X			X		Spectrum auctions	X		
Honduras		X	X		X					X				X	X		X				
Mexico		X		X	X					X	X		X	X			X	Virtual fund			
Nicaragua	X		X		X			X	X		X						X	Operator levy	X	X	
Peru	X		X		X			X	X	X	X					X		Operator levy	X[87]		
Venezuela	X		X		X	X		X	X	X	X					X		Operator levy	X	X	

77 Cooperatives with rural obligations
78 Multisectoral rural development fund supposed to also support rural telecoms, but is primarily used in other sectors
79 No obligations for the mirror license holders
80 Virtual telephony
81 Vast universal access program to support telecenters, distance learning, telemedicine applications
82 To ensure the viability, payphone operators are planning to charge higher interconnection fees
83 Only long distance operators
84 In addition to rural telephony and semi-urban telecenters, the fund will support distance learning and telemedicine applications
85 Privately financed
86 Guatel (the non-privatized remnant of the public network after Telgua's privatization), operates a rural network
87 Incumbent not eligible for funds, although it has access obligations in its license and is the major contributor to the fund

REGION/Country	US/UA definition		US/UA focus		US/UA OBLIGATIONS				RETAIL SCHEME				FUNDING MECHANISM						ALLOCATION OF US/UA FUNDS		
ASIA	Y	N	Rural	General	Incumbent	Cellular	Regional	Special rural license	Special pay phone operators	Phone shops & private PCOs	Telecenters	Innovative initiatives	Cross-subsidies	Interconnect fees	US/UA Fund N	US/UA Fund Y	US/UA Fund Plan	Funded through	Carriers	Retailers	Subscribers
Bangladesh	X		X		X	X		X		X		X[88]					X	Operator levy	X		
China		X			X								X		X						
India	X		X		X[89]					X	X		X				X	Operator levy	X		
Indonesia	X		X		X		X			X	X	X[90]	X		X						
Malaysia	X		X		X	X				X				X		X		Operator levy	X		
Nepal	X		X		X[91]	X		X		X			X			X		Operator levy	X		
Philippines	X			X		X				X	X						X	Govt	X		
Sri Lanka	X		X		X	X			X	X							X	Govt	X		
Thailand	X		X		X					X			X		X		X	Operator levy	X		

88 GrameenBank provides micro-loans for mobile payphone entrepreneurs (mostly women)
89 All fixed service providers
90 Wartels (PCOs) with internet access
91 All basic service providers to allocate 15% of their total investment to rural areas

REGION/Country	US/UA definition		US/UA focus		US/UA OBLIGATIONS				RETAIL SCHEME				FUNDING MECHANISM						ALLOCATION OF US/UA FUNDS		
ECA[92] & MNA[93]	Y	N	Rural	General	Incumbent	Cellular	Regional	Special rural license	Special pay phone operators	Phone shops & private PCOs	Telecenters	Innovative Initiatives	Cross-subsidies	Interconnect fees	US/UA Fund N	Y	Plan	Funded through	Carriers	Retailers	Subscribers
Bulgaria	X			X	X				X				X		X						
Georgia	X			X	X		X[95]						X				X[94]	Operator levy	X		
Hungary	X			X	X											X		License fees			
Kyrgyz Republic	X			X	X							X[96]	X		X						
Latvia		X			X								X		X						
Poland	X				X		X[97]					X[98]	X			X	X[99]	Gov't, operator levy	X		
Romania	X			X	X		X[100]						X		X						
Russia Fed.		X											X		X						
Slovak Rep.		X			X								X		X						
Jordan		X			X[101]								X		X						
Morocco	X			X	X	X				X			X				X	Operator levy	X		

92 Europe and Central Asia
93 Middle East and North Africa
94 New amendments to the telecom law create fund
95 Local Telephone Operators (LTOs)
96 Special service packages for low-income subscribers unable to pay market prices
97 LTOs
98 Payphones for the disabled
99 Government financed fund created in 1991 to support incumbent connection of 8,000 locations. New competitive fund foreseen in new law but not effective yet
100 Each local Elektrosvyaz has a rural development plan, but financial situation does not allow investments
101 Universal service requirements will fall on both the incumbent and the new operator.

REGION/Country	US/UA definition		US/UA focus		US/UA OBLIGATIONS				RETAIL SCHEME				FUNDING MECHANISM						ALLOCATION OF US/UA FUNDS		
	Y	N	Rural	General	Incumbent	Cellular	Regional	Special rural license	Special pay phone operators	Phone shops & private PCOs	Telecenters	Innovative initiatives	Cross-subsidies	Interconnect fees	US/UA Fund N	US/UA Fund Y	US/UA Fund Plan	US/UA Fund Funded through	Carriers	Retailers	Subscribers
ADVANCED COUNTRIES																					
Australia	X			X	X		X[102]				X					X		Virtual fund, pay or play	X		
Canada	X			X[103]	X						X			X	X						
Finland		X		X	X	X	X						X[104]	X							X
Greece	X			X	X								X								
New Zealand	X			X	X	X					X		X	X		X		Virtual fund			
United Kingdom	X			X	X							X[105]		X			X	Virtual fund			X
United States	X			X	X		X	X[106]				X[107]	X	X		X		Operator levy[108]	X	X[109]	X

-71-

102 Australia's Ministry for Communications recently initiated a bidding process for the opening of competition in regional areas.
103 Operators are required to fulfill service requests, but are allowed to set prices according to the cost of providing the service.
104 Direct subscriber subsidies to needy persons
105 Service packages for low income subscribers
106 Rural cooperatives receive subsidies from Rural Electrification Fund (also known as RUS)
107 Special discounts for low-income consumers. See also allocation of funds
108 Primarily long distance operators. Fund administered by NGO
109 Libraries, schools, rural healthcare providers

ANNEX 3: UNIVERSAL ACCESS PROFILES OF SELECTED COUNTRIES

ARGENTINA

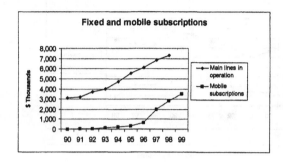

Fixed and mobile subscriptions

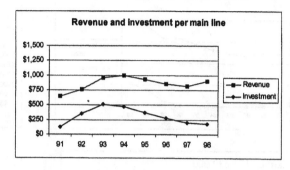

Revenue and investment per main line

Population: 35 677 000
Percent rural: 11.4 %
GDP per capita: $ 8950
Estimated rural per capita income: $1048
Telecom revenue as % of GDP: 1.7%
Fixed teledensity (per 100 people): 20.3
(per household): 64
Mobile teledensity: 7.8
Waiting list as % of fixed lines: 0.27%
Internet users per 10000 people: 83.05

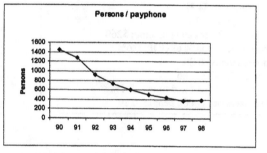

Persons / payphone

Privatization and liberalization

The incumbent Entel was privatized in 1990: Telecom Argentina and Telefonica de Argentina (TASA) were created with exclusive regional areas and a 7-year exclusivity (extended by 2 years).

Liberalization schedule:

Mobile services	1992
Local	Nov 1999
Long distance	Nov 1999
International services	Nov 2000

Regulatory agency: National Communications Commission (CNC) since 1990. The CNC works in partnership with the Secretariat of Communications (Secom) to determine the telecom policy.

Private service providers

* Four national long distance operators (duopoly in 2 regions), in 2000 three more licenses to be issued
* A number of independent operators, mostly co-operatives and rural
* Four dominant mobile operators
* Six PCS licenses issued in 1999, no new entrants
* In December 1998, two new pay phone concessions awarded totaling more than 10,000 public phones.

Universal service and rural telecommunications policies

The national universal service policy is under development. SECOM issued in March 1998 a decree with guidelines for the universal service definition.

License obligations to TELECOM and TASA include mandatory build-out targets, and the exclusivity period was extended based on reaching these targets.
The current obligations include the installation of:

* semi-public telephones (i.e. schools, libraries) in all communities with more than 80 residents
* 640,000 new lines in areas of more than 500 residents, and
* 19,000 new public telephones

Universal service / access finance

No special fund exists.

Internet Todos

Argentina Internet Todos project has been launched to finance 500 communications access centers throughout the country in schools, libraries, medical centers etc.

Comments and issues

The exclusivity period of the two regional incumbents was extended as they were able to perform successfully in reaching the service expansion targets.

Argentina has adopted a phased liberalization approach, where national and international long distance competition is introduced by restricting the number of new entrants to two.

The two new regional competitive operator consortiums include also rural co-operatives, and they profile their services partly as being rural.

BANGLADESH

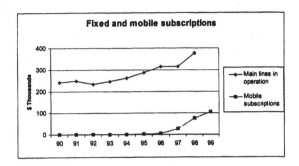

Fixed and mobile subscriptions

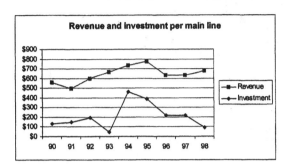

Revenue and investment per main line

Population: 123 630 000
Percent rural: 80.54 %
GDP per capita: $335
Estimated rural per capita income: $260
Telecom revenue as % of GDP: 0.6%
Fixed teledensity: 0.26
Mobile teledensity: 0.06
Waiting list as % of fixed lines: 49.1%
Internet users per 10000 people: 0.10

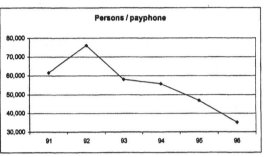

Persons / payphone

The incumbent Bangladesh Telegraph and Telephone Board (BTTB) is state-owned.

Liberalization schedule:

Mobile services	1989
Local	Rural 1989
Long distance	-
International services	-

Sector is regulated by the Ministry of Post and Telecommunications, no independent regulator exists.

Private service providers
- Two private operators with licenses to cover rural areas with exclusivity periods
- Four mobile licenses (one state-owned), a fifth license is to be issued in 1999/2000

The Bangladesh Rural Telecommunications Authority (BRTA) uses wireless technologies. The operator's ultimate plan is to install telecommunications services in 199 thanas out of a total of 460, and to provide one public payphone in every village in each of the thanas.

Universal service and rural telecommunications policies
The National Telecommunications Policy of 1998 promotes Universal Access as does the draft law. The policy promotes accessibility to all small administrative units (thanas), growth centers and villages by the year 2005.
The government has set the teledensity target to
- 4% by 2010, and
- to 10% by 2025.

The task of providing rural coverage is primarily the responsibility of the incumbent although there are two private operators with licenses to cover rural areas.

Universal service / access finance
The draft law includes no provisions for any special funding.

Grameen Phone
Grameen Phone is a rural arm of a GSM operator. Grameen Phone's target is to install
- at least one fixed cellular phone in each of the 68,000 villages.
- Grameen Phone service covers 750 villages.

The Grameenphone business case is based on giving micro-loans to low-income market segments. The company leases handsets to village women entrepreneurs who will in turn sell the service to the rest of the community. Community usage drives up airtime, and the entrepreneur is typically able to repay the loan within a few months. The village phone operator is responsible for extending services to customers for incoming and outgoing calls, collecting the call charges according to prescribed rates and maintaining the telephone set. The entrepreneur's net income consists of the difference between charges paid by the customers and the amount billed by the Village Phone administrators which includes air time and a flat charge for each incoming call.

Comments and issues
Grameen Phone has adopted very innovative approach to access expansion. The rural arm of Grameen Phone operates as a nonprofit organization.

Both fixed rural operators have complained that BTTB is holding back their operations by failing to provide interconnection. Interconnection is said to be unfair and uncertain and has led to slow rollout and poor financial performance.

BOTSWANA

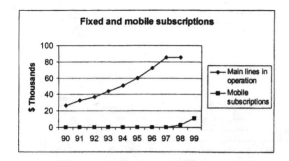

Fixed and mobile subscriptions

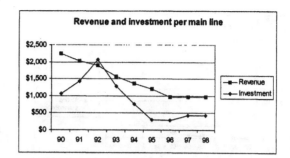

Revenue and investment per main line

Population: 1 533 000
Percent rural: 35 %
GDP per capita: 3307
Estimated rural per capita income
Telecom revenue as % of GDP: 1.7%
Fixed teledensity: 5.6 (per household 14.5)
Mobile teledensity: 0.19
Waiting list as % of fixed lines: 13.7%
Internet users per 10000 people: 63.69

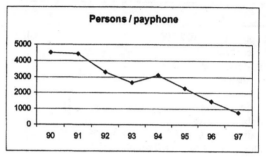

Persons / payphone

Privatization and liberalization

No timeframe for the privatization of the incumbent Botswana Telecommunications Corporation (BTC) is set. Private sector has been able to participate in all sectors (except operating the PSTN) since 1996. The duration of the BTC's monopoly over the national PSTN lies at the discretion of the government.

Liberalization schedule:
Mobile services   1996
Local   -
Long distance   -
International services   -
Regulatory Agency: the Botswana Telecommunications Authority (BTA) since 1996

Private service providers
• Two mobile operators since 1998

Universal service and rural telecommunications policies

One of the Telecommunications Policy's primary goals is universal service. The government has adopted a Rural Telecommunications Program which envisages the provision of telephony to villages of 500 people or more, a commitment which the BTC has adopted.

BTC has a project aiming to reach 160.000 access lines by 2001. A major part of the BTC's roll-out program concerns telephony in remote rural areas.

Mobile operators are obliged to install 500 public phones each in rural areas, within 4 years of starting their operations.

Virtual telephony

In 1998, BTC contracted an operator to build the necessary infrastructure for a fixed-line voice-messaging system or virtual telephony system. A year after the system has been set up, it will be taken over by BTC under a build-operate-transfer arrangement. Initially, the service will be aimed at those who are currently on the waiting list for telephones. 30,000 voice mailboxes will be installed at first. The owners of a mailbox will be able to dial into their voice mailbox and retrieve messages from any telephone.

Universal service / access finance

In the 1999/2000 national budget, some funds were allocated to subsidize BTC to extend coverage into villages in some regions in line with the Rural Telecommunications Program.

Comments and issues

The government of Botswana has utilized innovative approaches to enhance access in geographically challenging and sparsely populated areas. Fixed lines, multi-access radio, WLL technology, VSATs and virtual telephony are implemented to achieve this goal.

Operator obligations and some government funding are used as means to improve rural access, but if the government adopts a pro-competitive policy also in basic services, the benefits of competition would further expand rural access.

CHILE

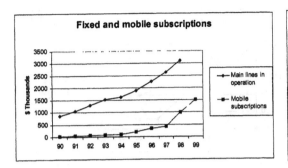

Fixed and mobile subscriptions

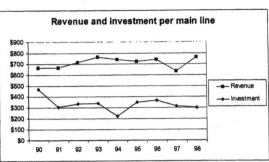

Revenue and investment per main line

Population: 14 622 000
Percent rural: 16 %
GDP per capita: $5272
Estimated rural per capita income: -
Telecom revenue as % of GDP: 2.2%
Fixed teledensity: 20.9 (per household 72.3)
Mobile teledensity: 6.7
Waiting list as % of fixed lines: 3.17%
Internet users per 10000 people: 202.37

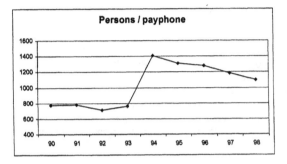

Persons / payphone

Privatization and liberalization
The incumbent Telefonica CTC Chile was privatized in 1988.

Liberalization schedule:

Mobile services	1989
Local	1989
Long distance	1994
International services	1994

Regulatory agency: SUBTEL

Private service providers
- 7 local operators
- 5 rural payphone operators
- 10 long distance operators
- 4 mobile operators
- 2 PCS licenses since 1996
- WLL licenses to be auctioned in 2000

Universal service / access finance
The Telecommunications Act 1994 establishes a Rural Telecommunication Development Fund to subsidize the installation of public telephones in marginal, low-income rural and urban areas.

The fund is administered by Subtel and financed through national budget. All operators are eligible to receive funds. Subsidies are distributed through competitive bidding, the bid evaluation emphasizes the lowest proposed subsidy combined with the commitment to short delivery time.

Rural payphone licenses are non-exclusive, and have service requirements in terms of the number of payphones and quality of service. Licenses give the right to install more lines than just the required payphones. Penalties are involved and even the threat of losing the license, if the targets are not met. Tariffs can also be set higher than in the urban areas, although the maximum tariff is set by the regulator.

The first competitive bidding was initiated in 1995, and the rural operators were selected in 1996. Subtel only distributed 48% of its budget in 1996 as 16 of the 46 suggested projects were awarded to operators that requested zero compensation. New rounds of competitive bidding are being arranged annually.

Comments and issues
The competitive bidding mechanism minimizes the use of subsidies, but some of the most challenging areas may not receive any bids and thus remain without service.

Some areas have been bid for zero subsidy and this has caused in some cases financial difficulties for the operators, resulting in service delays.

As an incentive, rural licensees have the right to install as many additional lines as seen feasible, as soon as the payphones are in place. This encourages further access enhancement if seen viable by the operators.

COLOMBIA

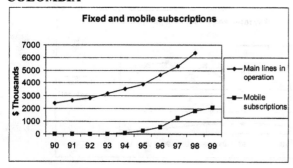

Fixed and mobile subscriptions

Main lines in operation
Mobile subscriptions

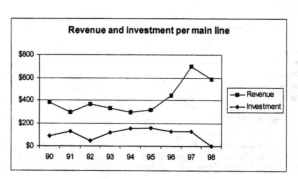

Revenue and investment per main line

Revenue
Investment

Population: 40 042 000
Percent rural: 26 %
GDP per capita: 2391
Estimated rural per capita income
Telecom revenue as % of GDP: 4.3%
Fixed teledensity: 17.6 (per household 66.2)
Mobile teledensity: 4.9
Waiting list as % of fixed lines: 12.6%
Internet users per 10000 people: 46.32

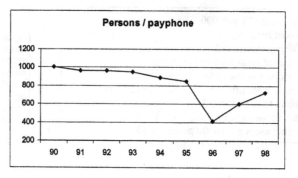

Persons / payphone

Privatization and liberalization
Liberalization has been pursued without privatization. The attempts to privatize the state owned long-distance and international service operator, Empresa Nacional de Telecomunicaciones (TELECOM) have failed.

Liberalization schedule:
Mobile services   1994
Local   1998
Long distance   Dec 1998
International services   Dec 1998
Regulatory Agency: The Telecommunications Regulatory Commission (CRT), MoC as well.

Private service providers
- 30 regional monopolies, state-owned
- Three long-distance operators
- TELECOM also operates a number of local companies and has formed alliances with others
- Six mobile operators, there are three regions each with a duopoly situation. The five-year exclusivity contracts expired in September 1999
- PCS introduced in 1999
- Two national LMDS (Local Multipoint Distribution Service) concessions as well as 17 regional concessions

The legislation allows free provision of WLL technology.

Consolidations or strategic alliances among both the fixed and mobile operators are probable in the future.

Universal service and rural telecommunications policies
The legislation defines universal access as providing telecom access within an acceptable distance to everyone.

In 1997, the government adopted a plan for 'social telephony' to promote and finance the unsatisfied demand in rural and urban areas. The plan projected to install 975,000 lines, one-third in urban areas and two-thirds in rural areas by the year 2000. Financing was to be provided by government funds (60%) and external sources (40%). However, the use of resources has not been carried out as projected. For example, in 1997, only US$26m was used to install just 12,300 lines in rural and urban areas.

New entrants in the long distance market (1998) are required to share social obligations with TELECOM.

Universal service/access finance
TELECOM and other long distance operators pay 5% of their revenues to a development fund.

Comments and issues
The urban teledensity in the 45 largest municipalities is verging on saturation. However, there are still at least 700 municipalities with teledensity of less than 5% and a further 176 without any service.

GHANA

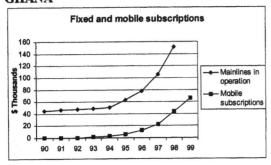

Fixed and mobile subscriptions

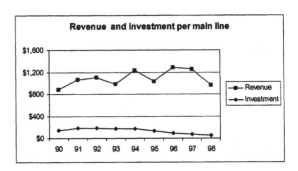

Revenue and investment per main line

Population: 17 985 000
Percent rural: 63 %
GDP per capita: 383
Estimated rural per capita income
Telecom revenue as % of GDP: 1.9%
Fixed teledensity: 0.57 (per household 1.57)
Mobile teledensity: 0.23
Waiting list as % of fixed lines: 19.66%
Internet users per 10000 people: 3.13

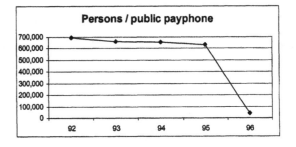

Persons / public payphone

Privatization and liberalization
The incumbent Ghana Telecom (GT) was privatized in 1997.

Liberalization schedule:

Mobile services	1992
Local	1997
Long distance	1997
International services	1997

Regulatory Agency: National Communications Authority since 1996.

Private service providers
- A Second National Operator license was issued in 1997. Duopoly situation remains until 2002.
- Four mobile operators (the second from 1995 onwards)
- A wireless rural operator

Universal service and rural telecommunications policies
Accelerated Development Programme (1994-99) objectives include:
- Provision of payphone facilities in urban and rural areas
- At least one payphone in every village of more than 500 people
- Mobile coverage to cover half the population, and in all the regional capitals

The following roll-out requirements are placed on the PSTN operators:
- The incumbent obligation is 275.000 main lines in 5 years
- The SNO requirement is 55.000 lines in 3 years

The mobile operator Celltel has a requirement to have 100.000 subscribers by 2001.

Regional rural license
ADP introduced the licensing of other operators to augment GT's roll-out plan. Additional providers of local services can be licensed to serve under-served population centers where the duopoly operators have declined rights of first refusal.

At the end of the five-year exclusivity period for the duopoly operators the government is committed to review whether to license additional national operators.

In 1994, a rural license was issued to Capital Telecom to provide, under franchise, service to the rural southern part of the country. CT began service in February 1997, initially providing 10,000 lines using Wireless Local Loop (WLL).

Universal service/access finance
Ghana Investment Fund for Telecommunications GIFTEL. In order to finance the provision of communication service in non-commercial areas and to promote education, training and research in the telecom sector, the licensees (fixed) must pay GIFTEL 1% of its net revenue.

Comments and issues
The government promotes telephone penetration and access by using wireless technology. The country has pro-competitive policies but progress towards real competition and rural access has been hindered by slow development and by limited effectiveness of the regulator.

HUNGARY

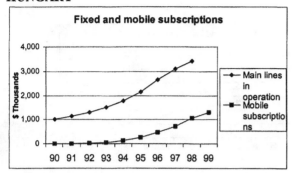

Fixed and mobile subscriptions

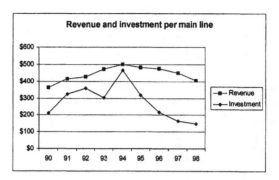

Revenue and investment per main line

Population: 10 155 000
Percent rural: 34 %
GDP per capita: 4503
Estimated rural per capita income
Telecom revenue as % of GDP: 3.1%
Fixed teledensity: 30.4 (per household 77)
Mobile teledensity: 10.5
Waiting list as % of fixed lines: 1.2%
Internet users per 10000 people:294.35

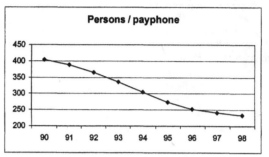

Persons / payphone

Privatization and liberalization

The incumbent Matav was privatized in 1993 with an exclusivity period until 2002. The negotiations with Matav are underway to end the exclusivity one year early, in 2001.

Liberalization schedule:

Mobile services	1994
Local	2002
Long distance	2002
International services	2002

Telecommunications is regulated by the Ministry of Transport, Telecommunications and Water Management (MTTW). Non-independent Communications Authority of Hungary performs the administrative functions and reports directly to the Ministry.

Private service providers

- Several regional monopoly operators. In 1995, the ownership of the 54 local networks previously operated by Matav were transferred to Local Telephone Operators (LTOs) for an 8-year exclusivity period, but Matav continued to hold 39 of the licenses. Two dominant LTOs have emerged, both operating in four or five regions.
- Four mobile operators, three of which have both GSM and DCS1800 licenses
- LMDS auctions are planned in 2000

Universal service and rural telecommunications policies

There are growth obligations for concessionaires, but no specific rural targets. The new Communications Law due to be introduced in 2001 will address the universal access requirements.

Local operators are required to achieve 15.5% annual increase in the number of main lines in the first six years, and to reduce the waiting period for a telephone line. Also, from January 1997, 90% of the telephone requests must be fulfilled within six months.

The Act on Telecommunications 1992 includes provision of public telecommunications services for disabled people. Also, the installation of a public telephone station for the purpose of safety of life and of property may not be refused by the service provider if the customer or the local government concerned assumes to cover the costs of installation of such station.

Universal service/ access finance

The funding possibilities of universal service are still under study.

Comments and issues

Matav remains a dominant player, its market share in the fixed-line sector remains above 90%.

Regional monopolies have achieved good results in improving teledensity, but the revenue sharing arrangements with Matav are not favorable for the LTOs.

The revenue sharing agreements require the regional operators to pay a significant part of their revenues to Matav as interconnect charges for long distance and international calls. Matav retains one-third of the revenues on calls originating from the LTOs and two-thirds on all calls received by the LTOs. To meet the build-out requirements, LTOs have started to utilize WLL technology.

INDIA

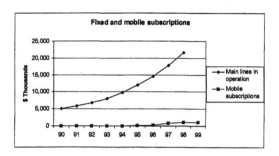

Fixed and mobile subscriptions

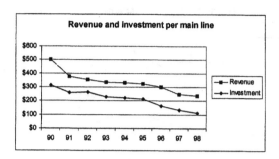

Revenue and investment per main line

Population: 962 380 000
Percent rural: 73 %
GDP per capita: 396
Estimated rural per capita income
Telecom revenue as % of GDP: 1.2%
Fixed teledensity: 1.86 (per household 8.6)
Mobile teledensity: 0.11
Waiting list as % of fixed lines: 12.5%
Internet users per 10000 people: 5.09

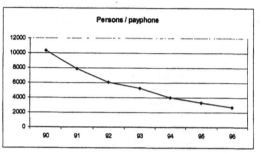

Persons / payphone

Privatization and liberalization

The incumbent Department of Telecommunications is partly state-owned. DoT is in effect part of the Ministry of Communications.

Liberalization schedule:

Mobile services	1994
Local	1994
Long distance	2000, delayed
International services	2004

Regulatory agency: The Telecommunication Regulatory Authority of India TRAI, since 1997. The TRAI Act was Amended 1/2000 so that the dispute settlement function is held by a separate Telecom Disputes Settlement and Appellate Tribunal. TRAI's role in spectrum allocation and interconnection arrangements is strengthened.

Private service providers

- Three partly state-owned fixed line operators
- 6 regional fixed local service licensees since 1996, 3 of which are operational
- In the mobile sector there are two service providers in most districts.

Universal service and rural telecommunications policies

The New Telecom Policy 1999 (NTP99) deals with India's Universal Service Obligation and the Universal Service Fund.
The Government seeks to achieve the following universal service objectives:

- Provide voice and low speed data service to the remaining 290,000 uncovered villages by the year 2002
- Achieve Internet access to all district head quarters by the year 2000, and
- Achieve telephone on demand in urban and rural areas by 2002

The license requirements for the new entrants in basic services include:

- Providing a fixed amount of Direct Exchange Lines (DELs) during the first three years, and a fixed growth rate thereafter
- A fixed proportion (10%) of the DELs has to be allocated to village public telephones (VPTs).

The mobile operators are allowed to operate cellular or fixed payphones.

There are Public Call Offices provided by both the fixed an mobile operators. DoT operates currently 340,566 Village Public Telephones and 520,680 PCOs.

Universal service / access finance

All operators under various licenses are required to contribute a percentage of their revenue into the fund, the percentage is not yet decided. The USO obligation is borne by all fixed service providers who are reimbursed from the fund. Other operators who provide universal service will also be eligible for funding.

Comments and issues

The regulatory framework has not convinced private investors.

The regulatory agency's jurisdiction power over DoT is controversial as the incumbent is at the same time an operator and a governmental body. This has severely deterred introduction of competition. For instance, interconnection agreements were drawn up by DoT to the disadvantage of its competitors. Now TRAI's role is strengthened in both interconnection and spectrum allocations.

MALAYSIA

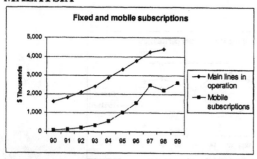

Fixed and mobile subscriptions

- Main lines in operation
- Mobile subscriptions

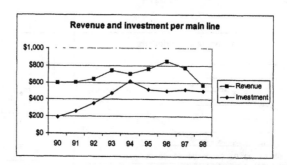

Revenue and investment per main line

- Revenue
- Investment

Population: 21 667 000
Percent rural: 45 %
GDP per capita: $4545
Estimated rural per capita income: $4066
Telecom revenue as % of GDP: 3.3%
Fixed teledensity: 19.76 (per household 71.5)
Mobile teledensity: 7.5
Waiting list as % of fixed lines: 3.7%
Internet users per 10000 people: 360.66

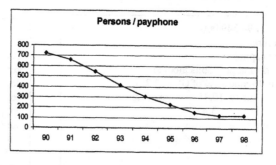

Persons / payphone

Privatization and liberalization
The incumbent Telekom Malaysia was privatized in 1990.

Liberalization schedule:

Mobile services	1989
Local	1994
Long distance	1994
International services	1994

Regulatory agency: The Malaysian Communications and Multimedia Commission, a new government body charged with regulating Malaysia's entire telecoms and multimedia industries since April 1999.

Private service providers
- 5 fixed line operators with rights to provide also international call services
- 7 licensed mobile operators (5 of them are also fixed operators)

Universal service and rural telecommunications policies
The law of 1998 includes a universal service definition and provisions for establishing a Universal Service Provision fund, the "USP".

The teledensity objective is 50 main lines per 100 inhabitants, with a minimum of 25 lines per 100 people in rural areas by 2020.

The incumbent's goal is to achieve:
- a high residential penetration in many rural communities, and
- at least one payphone in each of the country's over 17.000 villages

Universal service / access finance
Telekom Malaysia will remain the sole Universal Service Obligations (USO) operator for an interim period of two years, with costs recovered via an USO charge on all interconnecting traffic. Following the interim period, which took effect from January 1999, operators who agree to roll out services to the under-serviced areas will be compensated for losses from the USO fund.

The fixed and mobile operators share these USOs including fixed contributions (2% of annual revenues) to the USP fund. Services included in the USO are basic telephony, public telephones and services for the disabled.

Comments and issues
The aggressive rural telecommunications policy is unique among developing countries. Malaysia is attempting the transition from pursuing universal access to universal service for its rural areas with relatively low per capita income level. The government's accelerated economic development plan (Vision 2020) has the goal of industrial country status and has rural development as a major element.

MEXICO

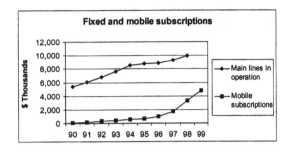

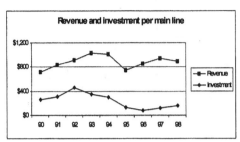

Population: 94 349 000
Percent rural: 26 %
GDP per capita: 4271
Estimated rural per capita income
Telecom revenue as % of GDP: 2.2%
Fixed teledensity: 10.35 (per household 37)
Mobile teledensity: 3.4
Waiting list as % of fixed lines: 2%
Internet users per 10000 people: 140.87

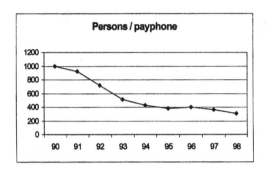

Privatization and liberalization
The incumbent Telmex was privatized in 1990.

Liberalization schedule:
Mobile services   1989
Local   1997
Long distance   1997
International   1997
Regulatory agency: Cofetel since 1995

Private service providers
- Mobile licenses in nine regions, however two dominant operators
- A large number of local/ long-distance operators
- WLL and PCS concessions auctioned to 8 operators in 1998

The dominant operators TELMEX and TELCEL will have to wait two years before deploying their respective WLL and PCS networks, as stipulated in regulations aimed at encouraging competition in the local loop.

Universal service and rural telecommunications policies
The Law of 1995 requires the MoCT to prepare programs for social and rural coverage to be performed by any concessionaire.

The incumbent license obligations included:
- By 1994 provision of payphones in 20,000 rural localities, i.e. in all communities with over 500 inhabitants

- By 1998 providing five public phones for every 1,000 people

Telmex has nearly reached its access targets, and the remaining target is to meet all service requests within one month.

The other licensed operators are required to meet coverage goals in their license areas.

Universal service / access finance
There is no universal service fund, although creation of one is under consideration. Cofetel is considering a "virtual fund" (interconnection mechanism) or a fund administered by the private sector.

Comments and issues
Encouraging line growth through license obligations has been successful with regard to the satisfactory performance of Telmex in meeting its access targets. In addition, the introduction of competition has also had a clear effect on telecommunications investments and has somewhat improved access by the poor and in rural areas.

However, Telmex continues to dominate virtually every service sector. Local competition has been nonexistent due to the heavy subsidization of local services. The interconnection regime is not transparent enough, nor is it cost based.

PERU

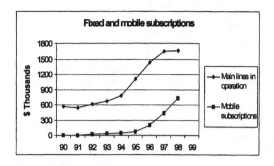

Population: 24 371 000
Percent rural: 28 %
GDP per capita: 2620
Estimated rural per capita income
Telecom revenue as % of GDP: 2.5%
Fixed teledensity: 6.75 (per household 27.7)
Mobile teledensity: 3.0
Waiting list as % of fixed lines: 3.1%
Internet users per 10000 people: 80.65

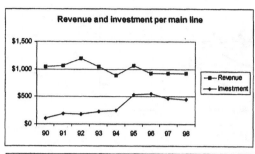

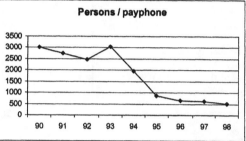

Privatization and liberalization
The incumbent Telefonica del Peru was privatized in 1994 with a five-year exclusivity period in fixed telephony. The monopoly ended one year ahead of schedule in 1998.

Liberalization schedule:

Mobile services	1998
Local	Aug 1998
Long distance	Aug 1998
International services	Aug 1998

Regulatory agency: OSIPTEL since 1993

Private service providers
- 23 long-distance operators
- Two local service providers in addition to the incumbent
- Three rural operators
- Three mobile licensees

Universal service and rural telecommunications policies
Peru has established a rural development fund for establishing public access centers in rural areas that are not included in Telefonica del Peru's universal service requirements.
Ministry of Transport and Communications' goals (1999) include the following:
- Increasing teledensity to 20%
- Establishing 5,000 public access centers in new localities by 2003

Telefonica del Peru is required to:
- install 1 million new lines,
- install 19,000 public pay phones (1 public payphone for each 500 people), and
- connect 1,486 population centers with more than 500 people to the public switched network.

The new entrants are required to install lines equivalent to 5% of the lines of the leading operator at the time of the concession

The long distance entrants are obliged to build up infrastructure in at least five cities with more than 50,000 inhabitants.

Universal service / access finance
The Fondo de Inversión en Telecomunicaciones (FITEL) was established in the 1993 Telecommunications Law. FITEL is administered by the regulator. The objective of the fund is to provide:
- public payphones in 5,000 rural towns with over 400 inhabitants and telecenters in all district capitals by the year 2003.

FITEL funds are collected through one percent tax on the gross revenues of all public telecommunications companies. The locations considered of priority social interest can receive finance from FITEL. Funds are allocated through public competitive bidding as in Chile.
Telefonica is not eligible to receive funds, although it is required to meet access goals through its license agreement.

Comments and issues
The first bidding round, considered a pilot, was issued in 1998 including 213 localities. The second and third bidding rounds in 1999 and 2000 covered three regions each, and a total of 1937 and 2290 localities, respectively. Every year a different company won the bids for all the regions tendered. So far, FITEL can be considered a successful experience.

Red Cientifica Peruana
RCP focuses on the low-end Internet market via cabinas publicas, small public telephone booths equipped with computers wired to the Internet. Currently there are about 500 wired booths, 47 of them operated by the RCP.

PHILIPPINES

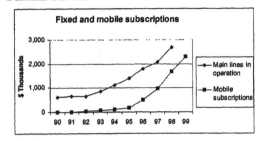

Fixed and mobile subscriptions

- Main lines in operation
- Mobile subscriptions

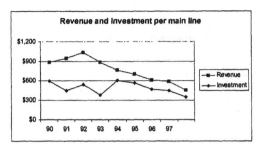

Revenue and investment per main line

- Revenue
- Investment

Population: 73 527 000
Percent rural: 44 %
GDP per capita: 1117
Estimated rural per capita income
Telecom revenue as % of GDP: 1.5%
Fixed teledensity: 2.86 (per household 11.9)
Mobile teledensity: 2.3
Waiting list as % of fixed lines: 33.3%
Internet users per 10000 people: 20.56

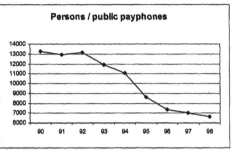

Persons / public payphones

Privatization and liberalization

The incumbent Philippines Long Distance Telephone Co. (PLDT) was privatized in 1998.

Liberalization schedule:

Mobile services	1993
Local	1993
Long distance	1993
International services	1993

Regulatory agency: National Telecommunications Commission (NTC) since 1979, under the direct authority of the Department of Transport and Communications.

Private sector providers

- 69 private local exchange carrier operators, four inter-exchange carrier operators, and nine international gateway facilities operators
- Five mobile operators, plans to issue PCS licenses still under consideration by the NTC

Universal service and rural telecommunications policies

Under the Service Area Scheme (SAS), the licensed international gateway and mobile operators had service obligations. Each operator was provided with a monopoly territory. All mobile operators were required to install a minimum of 400,000 telephone lines, whilst international operators must establish 300,000 land-lines by April 1998 (totaling 2 million lines). The key objective of the SAS was to have at least one rural line installed for every ten urban lines.

Universal service /access finance

Philippines has plans to set up a Universal Access Fund. The local carriers can be paid subsidies from the fund for their roll-out in the rural areas of the country.

The results of SAS

By the end of 1998, most operators had not met their obligation but over 1 million rural lines were installed. Despite the steep increase in rural teledensity, many villages still lacked access to basic telephone service.

No business and residential split was specified and the carriers have overlooked the high-cost areas. The SAS has now been completed and additional development of lines will be left to competitive forces.

According to official statistics, the main line capacity in 1998 was 6,699,919 lines but out of those there are only 2,700,000 main lines in operation.

Municipal Public Calling Office Program

A separate Municipal Public Calling Office Program aims at providing rural and remote municipalities and communities (baranguays) with public calling office telephony access. Capital costs are covered by government loans and grants. The program has now been extended to community telecenters.

Comments and issues

SAS was not technology neutral. Operators were required to rollout fixed wireline telephony services. As a result, wireless technologies have not been employed.

The model promotes subsidizing local service provision with revenues from cellular and international services.

A more refined system would have given investors targets for specific rural zones and villages, and thus enhanced the access for the poor and rural people.

PLTD still has over 60% of the market share. High interconnection charges by the PLDT have made the provision of fixed lines by other LECs uneconomical and thus they concentrate in enhancing their mobile operations. Service affordability and fast mobile subscription take-up /substitution is affecting the growth in mainlines.

The NTC has proposed granting of a national license to the operators who previously were assigned specific service areas.

POLAND

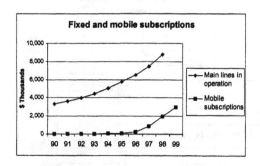

Fixed and mobile subscriptions

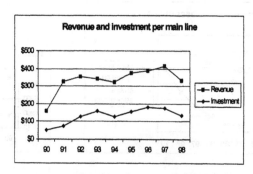

Revenue and investment per main line

Population: 38 650 000
Percent rural: 36 %
GDP per capita: 3510
Estimated rural per capita income
Telecom revenue as % of GDP: 2.3%
Fixed teledensity: 22.76 (per household 56.1)
Mobile teledensity: 5.0
Waiting list as % of fixed lines: 26.4%
Internet users per 10000 people: 408.34

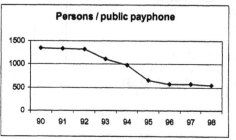

Persons / public payphone

Privatization and liberalization
The incumbent TPSA's privatization began in October 1998 with a 30% stake. Further privatization of 35% stake was completed in late 2000.

Liberalization schedule:
Mobile services   1996
Local   1991
Long distance   End of 1999
International services   2003
Regulator: Ministry of Communications (MoC)

Private service providers
- Approximately 45 local operators in competition with TPSA. In the Warsaw region there are two licensed operators to compete with the incumbent. Some of the local operators are managed as community cooperatives and/or in cooperation with local government bodies.
- There are five major local operators that each hold several local licenses. LTOs are allowed to operate WLL
- Three long-distance license holders
- Three mobile operators.

Universal service and rural telecommunications policies
Poland's telecommunications policy goals include improving universal access as well as encouraging competition. The new law, approved in 2000, has provisions for setting up of an independent regulatory body and specific provisions on a universal service.

The public operator with the highest market share in the area where universal service requirements are not met can be obliged by the Office of Telecom Regulations to provide the service.

The new law also establishes a delivery deadline for the universal service obligation - if a customer asks for a line, the operator is obliged to provide one within 30 days or face a penalty.

Universal service/access finance
A proposal exists to create a Universal Service Fund, which will collect annual contributions from operators with annual revenues exceeding EURO 2 million.

The Fund would pay subsidies to the eligible operators applying for subsidies.

Comments and issues
In 1991 there were 4,500 villages without access, the number decreased to 881 by June 1997. Poland had a special program between 1991-96 to install at least one telephone line in each locality without service.

Despite competition, TPSA still dominates most of the local market.

Fixed local licenses have not improved rural access significantly. High interconnection charges and unbalanced tariffs, as well as high concession fees hinder competition. Consolidation of small local operators can be expected in the future.

SOUTH AFRICA

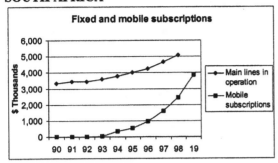

Fixed and mobile subscriptions

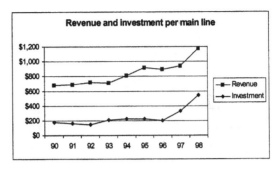

Revenue and investment per main line

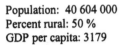

Population: 40 604 000
Percent rural: 50 %
GDP per capita: 3179
Estimated rural per capita income
Telecom revenue as % of GDP: 3.4%
Fixed teledensity: 10.71 (per household 33)
Mobile teledensity: 5.5
Waiting list as % of fixed lines: 2.3%
Internet users per 10000 people: 285.75

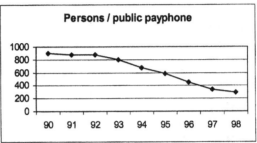

Persons / public payphone

Privatization and liberalization

The incumbent Telkom was privatized in 1997, with a 5-year exclusivity in voice services that can be extended if Telkom meets its build-out obligations.

Liberalization schedule:

Mobile services	1993
Local	2003
Long distance	2003
International services	2003

Regulatory agency: SATRA

Private service providers

- Three cellular operators

Universal service and rural telecommunications policies

The telecommunications law targets nationwide universal service by 2000.

- The incumbent requirements include basic services and public payphone service:
- 1,7 million mainlines in disadvantaged areas
- 120,000 payphones and lines to 20,000 priority customers and to 3,204 villages by 2002

If it meets 90% of the total roll-out and at least 80% of the under-served area roll-out, an extra year of exclusivity may be awarded on the condition that the total and underserved area roll-out targets are increased. Financial penalties are imposed if the targets are not met.

Cellular operators are required to install:

- 29,500 community public telephones within 5 years in under-served areas

They are obliged to use mobile technology to reach their targets. Call prices for cellular community phones are tariffed at less than half the standard cellular charge.

Universal service/ access finance

The new legislation establishes the Universal Service Agency (USA), separate from SATRA, that will manage the universal service fund. Every licensee makes an annual contribution of 0.16% of the annual turnover. Subsidies are disbursed only to telecenter operators.

USA

USA identifies and administers "creative and innovative methods" to promote universal service. It has currently established 18 full telecentres, 10 mini-telecentres and 30 full telecentres.

Comments and issues

Telkom's challenging roll-out targets have caused exceptionally high (70%) customer churn especially in rural areas. Many newly connected households cannot afford the bills and are disconnected.

The increasing number of cellular subscriptions and the affordability threshold limit Telkom's success in achieving its build-out requirements.

UGANDA

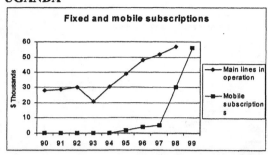

Fixed and mobile subscriptions

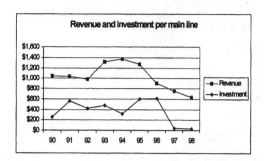

Revenue and investment per main line

Population: 20 317 000
Percent rural: 87 %
GDP per capita: 324
Estimated rural per capita income
Telecom revenue as % of GDP: 0.6%
Fixed teledensity: 0.26 (per household 0.43)
Mobile teledensity: 0.15
Waiting list as % of fixed lines: 11%
Internet users per 10000 people: 1.95

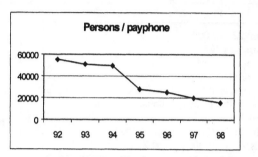

Persons / payphone

Privatization and liberalization
Privatization of the incumbent Uganda Telecommunications Limited (UTL) failed in 1998, but was successfully concluded in 2000. A Second National Operator was licensed in 1998.

Liberalization schedule:
Mobile services   1995
Local   April 1998
Long distance   April 1998
International services   April 1998
Regulatory agency: Uganda Communications Commission since 1996.

Private service providers
- Second National operator, owner of which is a foreign cellular operator
- Three mobile operators, including the incumbent.

Universal service and rural telecommunications policies
The 1996 Policy Statement objectives are to
- Increase teledensity from 0.25 to 2.0 lines per 100 people by 2000,
- Reduce waiting time, and
- Increase the geographical distribution of telecommunications services

Access expansion is achieved through roll-out obligations in the licenses for the major operators and where this is not possible, through establishing and utilizing a fund.

Both the fixed and mobile licensees have build-out obligations.
- The incumbent build-out requirement is 100.000 lines in 5 years

- The SNO requirement was originally 60.000 although the winning bidder committed to build 89.000 lines

The SNO bid evaluation criteria included network roll-out commitment in addition to the bid price. The SNO license allows MTN to also offer mobile cellular services, and it aims at meeting the roll-out target using GSM technology rather than fixed lines.

Universal service/ access finance
The Rural Communications Development Fund (RCDF), created by the 1997 law to support rural communications, is funded by contributions of up to 2.5% of operators' gross revenues, though currently they are only required to pay 1%. Licensing special rural operators is under consideration.

The incumbent UTL has developed a Pilot Rural Telecommunications Project, which could be funded by the RCDF.

UTL development plan
The UTL development plan for 1999/2000 included:
- provision of mobile and fixed cellular services (WLL technology) to meet the increasing demand, and
- tele-shops and multipurpose community telecenters and provision of Internet service.

Comments and issues
Both national operators are allowed to benefit from fixed and mobile convergence in a challenging terrain.

The drop in main lines in 1993 was due to a network verification program, where UPTC disconnected the lines of all delinquent subscribers.

VENEZUELA, REPUBLICA BOLIVARIANA

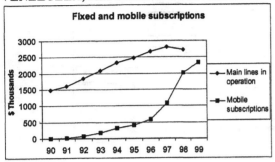

Fixed and mobile subscriptions

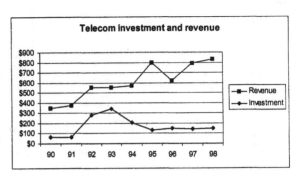

Telecom investment and revenue

Population: 22 777 000
Percent rural: 14 %
GDP per capita: $ 3841
Estimated rural per capita income: $ 826
Telecom revenue as % of GDP: 2.6%
Fixed teledensity: 11.66 (per household 45.8)
Mobile teledensity: 8.7
Waiting list as % of fixed lines: 14.5%
Internet users per 10000 people: 21.51

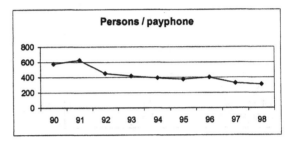

Persons / payphone

Privatization and liberalization
The incumbent CANTV was privatized in 1991.

Liberalization schedule:

Mobile services	1991
Local	Nov 2000
Long distance	Nov 2000
International services	Nov 2000

Regulatory agency: CONATEL is directly under the supervision of the Ministry of Transport and Communications.

Private service operators
- Three licensed regional fixed-line operators since 1998, which are also allowed to provide mobile services and have formed a third nationwide mobile operator
- Two nationwide mobile operators.

Universal service and rural telecommunications policies
The new Telecommunications Law, issued in 2000, created a universal service fund.

CANTV has payphone and line installation requirements in its concession agreement. Towards the year 2000,
- 85.000 payphones, and
- 3.75 million mainlines should be in place

- After the privatization CANTV was required to extend basic telephony to rural areas, defined as towns with less than 5,000 inhabitants.

Regional rural operators
Followed by CANTV's inability to meet its rural obligations, three regional rural operators were licensed. The existing operators were not allowed to tender for licenses. These regional operators are required to provide service in rural areas –including public phones and fixed or mobile lines- not covered by CANTV. In five years the operator specific build-out targets are 17.000, 42.000 and 38.000 lines respectively.

Universal service/access finance
The universal service fund is financed through contributions by operators of 1% of turnover.

Comments and issues
To make the rural licenses attractive, licenses allow operators to offer fixed access, long-distance, international, mobile and multimedia services.

The existing operators have criticized that they were not allowed to participate in tendering for these licenses.

Interconnection between the competing operators and CANTV has proven to be difficult. With more effective regulations, regional rural licenses would improve access significantly faster.

ANNEX 4: METHODOLOGY FOR COUNTRY GROUPINGS

A two dimensional *descriptive* model was developed to classify countries in terms of their degree of telecommunications liberalization thus far and their level of geo-economic challenge. Altogether, sixty countries were analyzed and studied.

The model shows four degrees of market liberalization and three levels of geo-economic challenge, which might affect decisions on specific liberalization strategies (especially for rural areas) and the license conditions to be set by the regulatory agency. Facilitating profitable service provision in challenging areas requires special attention and creation of incentives to increase the attractiveness of these areas to private investments as well as to facilitate the commercial viability of operations.

DEGREE OF LIBERALIZATION

The first dimension of the model is the degree of liberalization, divided into four stages:

- Monopoly environment in fixed and mobile services,
- Monopoly in fixed but competition in mobile services, and most often also in other market segments, such as value-added services and sometimes pay phones,
- Partial liberalization, where only some segments of the fixed telephony market remain under monopoly provision, typically domestic long-distance and international telephony,
- Fully competitive environment.

DEGREE OF GEOECONOMIC CHALLENGE

This dimension reflects the degree of geographic and economic challenge. Geographic challenge reflects the ratio of remote and challenging rural areas compared with the total surface area of the country. Economic challenge describes the income level and the level of economic disparity in the country. Four basic indicators were used to derive the level of geo-economic challenge:

- GDP per capita (the higher the lower the challenge)
- Gini index (economic disparity, the larger the index, the more challenging)
- Ratio of total land per arable and crop land (reflecting the possibly mountainous or deserted areas and with sparse population)
- Geographic size (area) of the country

With each of the indicators, the countries were grouped according to a four-scale rating based on pre-set limits. In the rating system, number 4 represents the highest challenge, and number 1 the lowest challenge. The limits for the four-scale rating for each indicator are presented in the following table.

The principle applied in setting the limits is to form approximately similar sizes of country groups and to look for 'natural' break points – e.g. between the very lowest and low-medium income countries. The selection is to some extent a subjective 'best judgment'.

Table A-4.1. Individual geoeconomic challenge ratings

Rating	ECONOMIC INDICATORS		GEOGRAPHIC INDICATORS	
	Gini-index	GDP per capita	Surface area	Total area/ crop+arable land
4	50-60	less than $350	Above 1 200 000	Ratio of 20 to 205
3	40-49,9	$351 - $1 000	401 000 – 1 200 000	Ratio of 10 to 19
2	30- 39,9	$1 001 - $4 000	151 000 – 400 000	Ratio of 5 to 9
1	less than 30	more than $4 000	10 000 - 150 000	Ratio of 1 to 4

Economic indicators

The Gini index represents the economic disparity of the country. The index measures the extent which the distribution of income among individuals and households within an economy deviates from a perfectly equal distribution. The higher the Gini index, the greater economic disparity a country has. A Gini index of zero represents perfect equality, while an index of 100 implies perfect inequality. Among the panel countries the indexes range from 19 to 60.

Some countries were lacking the Gini index, and they were given an estimated rating based on the level of Gini index in the countries with similar economic conditions. For example, Argentina is estimated to have approximately the same income distribution difference as Paraguay.

Gross Domestic Product per capita affects the affordability threshold of telecommunication services. The higher the GDP is in the country, the more money people can afford to spend on telecommunication services and thus greater share of population can be reached via commercial service provisioning.

GDP per capita ranges from Niger's less than $200, to $30,000 in the United States.

Geographic indicators

Total surface area among the panel countries ranges from 11,000 square km to nearly 10 million square km. The total surface area as an indicator implies that a country with a large surface area is more likely to have a greater proportion of high cost rural and remote areas than a geographically smaller country.

Ratio of total land area divided by arable and crop land area defines the land use of the country and thus gives an indication of how dispersed the population is.

According to the WDI, the definition of arable land includes land under temporary meadows for mowing or for pasture, land under market or kitchen gardens, and land temporarily fallow. Permanent crop land, on the other hand, is land cultivated with crops that occupy the land for long periods. This category includes land under flowering shrubs, fruit trees, nut trees, and vines, but excludes land under trees grown for wood or timber.

Ratio of total land area divided by combined area of arable and crop land ranges from 1,5 in Bangladesh to the ratio of 205 in Mauritania. For example, in Mauritania only 0.5% of the total land area is arable or used as crop land. As population clusters tend to form in arable areas suitable for cultivation, the less there is arable land, the more dispersed the population tends to be which then affects the costs of telecommunications to the more challenging areas.

Aggregated indicator for geoeconomic challenge

The four indicators were aggregated into a combined challenge score by calculating the weighted average with each indicator given the same weight (0.25).

Based on the aggregated geo-economic challenge scores ranging from 0.5 to 4.0, panel countries were divided into three classes, now representing the country Groups 1, 2 and 3.

In the following table the ranges for the aggregated geo-economic challenge scores are given for each country group:

Table A-4.2. Aggregate geoeconomic challenge ratings

Countries	Range of aggregated indicator
Group 3	4.00 – 2.75
Group 2	2.50 – 2.00
Group 1	0.75 – 1.75

Based on this rating, a three level challenge classification was derived:

- *Group 1: Uniform, densely populated and/or small country*

  Country with little regional variation because of small size and/or topographic simplicity. Rural and urban differences, however, might still be high, with regard to both population density and economic inequality.

- *Group 2: Significant regional variation*

  Country with major regional variation, with some regions providing significant challenge for the telecommunications cost structure due to geographic extremes. The country's economic inequalities may also be significant.

- *Group 3: Remote and challenging areas*

  Typically the size of the country is large and topography is challenging (mountainous or islands) and thus requires special technology and investments to provide service coverage. Economic disparity between geographic areas is significant.

COUNTRY GROUPS

Based on the two dimensions just described, each country can be placed visually within a grid showing its current status, as shown in the table below:

Table A-4.3. Country categories on liberalization and geoeconomic dimensions

Liberalization/ Challenge rating	Monopoly	Only mobile competition	Partially liberal	Open market
GROUP 3 Remote areas and/or high economic disparity	Nepal ▶	Burkina Faso Chad Kenya ▶ Mozambique Niger Senegal South Africa	Angola Bolivia ▶ Brazil ▶ China Indonesia Mali Mauritania Nigeria ▶ Russia Tanzania Venezuela ▶	Argentina Australia Canada Chile Colombia Madagascar Mexico Peru U.S.
GROUP 2 Significant variations	Gambia Nicaragua ▶	Botswana Bulgaria Cote d'Ivoire Ecuador ▶ Jordan Morocco Romania ▶	Ghana Honduras India ▶ Kyrgyz Rep. Sri Lanka Thailand	Dominican Rep. Finland Guatemala Malaysia Philippines Uganda
GROUP 1 Uniform, densely populated and/or small country		Gabon Greece Hungary ▶ ▶ Latvia Malawi Slovak Rep.	Bangladesh Poland ▶ Togo	El Salvador Georgia New Zealand UK

▶ indicates that the country is moving toward the next liberalization stage in the near future. A double arrow indicates that the scale of change will amount to a 'leapfrogging' of one stage.

ANNEX 5: METHODOLOGY TO APPROXIMATE UNIVERSAL ACCESS COSTS

OVERALL APPROACH

This annex tries to establish a simple rule of thumb for estimating an approximate amount of WB financing for the initial start-up of universal access funds, wherever this may be warranted. The results are attached as a table at the end of this annex and are meant to be indicative, requiring more detailed analysis before they can be applied in a specific operation.

The same sixty-two sample countries used throughout the paper were analyzed, representing all regions, including seven advanced industrialized countries for reference purposes.

The simplified methodology used assumes that all urban population is already somehow covered in terms of access to basic public telephone service (within reasonable walking distance), while it is assumed that all rural population has still to be served. In addition, telecenters with Internet access are assumed not yet to be available to either urban or rural population.

A uniform definition of universal access has been applied for all sample countries. While it is recognized that this may not give a realistic picture of UA costs and financing requirements when taking into account the different levels of development and telecommunications infrastructure in different regions and in specific countries, the methodology is simple enough to allow fine-tuning in accordance with the desired level of universal access and the actual situation in the country (including actual coverage of the telecommunications network, electricity and transport infrastructures, population density, demand for access to telephones and Internet, and existing universal access mechanisms, among others).

METHODOLOGY AND COST ESTIMATES

Table A-5.1 provides an indicative estimate of the investment and external financing required in the sample countries to meet a commonly defined set of "reference" universal access objectives within a five-year period. The following assumptions were made:

- Universal access objectives and unit costs are defined as follows: it is assumed that one public telephone is to be provided for every 1,000 rural dwellers[110] at a unit cost of US$ 5,000, while one telecenter is to be provided for every 50,000 people in the country (both rural and urban) at a unit cost of $50,000[111].
- Annual contributions into a hypothetical universal access fund are assumed to be equal to 1% of overall telecommunications sector revenue, which is a typical value of the Universal Service Levy (USL) in many countries surveyed.
- The amount of private finance leveraged through the competitive allocation of funds was assumed to be at least 40% of the project costs, thereby requiring a maximum 60% investment subsidy from the fund.

---

[110] This round number is used for convenience, approximately representing the average size of a target rural community (defined, for instance, in terms of reasonable walking distance). In many countries a portion of the rural population may already have access to basic telephone service and the average size of rural communities may be substantially lower or higher than 1,000, so adjustments to this figure would have to be made, as explained below.
[111] These are average costs. In some countries actual investment costs may be higher due to the need for expansion of the backbone network, provision of satellite hub station and terminals or need for alternative sources of energy. In particular, solar-powered satellite terminals (VSAT) may cost two to three times as much as terminals powered with existing power sources.

Based on these assumptions, the total investment cost of meeting the above universal access objectives was estimated both for public pay phones providing access to basic telephone service and telecenters providing public Internet access. This further allowed us to estimate the number of years required to meet these universal access objectives relying only on finance from the USL and the private finance leveraged through the competitive process. For countries where meeting these objectives would take longer than five years, an additional external financing required to meet the objectives within a five-year period was estimated.

RESULTS OF THE ANALYSIS

The results of this analysis, as summarized in Table A-5.1, indicate that in countries with moderate levels of network development, the above universal access targets are probably underestimated, and more aggressive targets could be envisioned. On the other hand, in countries with a limited telecommunications infrastructure and marginal sector revenues, the relatively small USL of 1 % cannot support high levels of universal access, such as in Bangladesh, India (at least in part), Nepal and many Sub-Saharan African countries. These countries will require a combination of many of the policies described in the paper, in particular opening of the markets, in addition to a more realistic definition of universal access, a somewhat larger USL (at least in the beginning) and some initial donor support to jump-start universal access fund implementation.

Large countries with an extensive telecommunications infrastructure e.g. China, Russia and possibly India, already have quite extensive terrestrial backbone and rural networks providing basic access to part of the rural population and have a reasonable telecommunications revenue to support some level of universal access. Accordingly it might be less expensive to provide basic access to the remaining population than indicated in the table and less external financing might be needed in these countries than estimated.

In terms of priorities for WB involvement, this analysis suggests that the highest priority countries for WB financing of universal access subsidies would be in Asia and Africa, assuming other conditions described elsewhere in the paper are met, notably Bangladesh, India, Nepal, Burkina Faso, Chad, Madagascar, Malawi, Mozambique, Niger, Tanzania and Uganda. A lower degree of WB financing, but with equally dramatic impact, may be required in Latin America, ECA[112] and MNA[113], notably in Nicaragua, Honduras, Guatemala, Georgia, Kyrgyz Republic, Romania and Morocco (among the sample countries).

THE COST OF NOT REFORMING

A related result of this analysis is that not reforming the telecommunications sector has a measurable cost. By calculating on a per capita basis the total cost of the reference universal access objectives described above, it is possible to show that it is much more expensive to bridge the digital divide in countries that have introduced few reforms than in countries that have adopted a decisive pro-competitive stance. As summarized in table A-5.2, the sample countries that are still part of the "monopoly" group require on average $5 per capita to implement the reference universal access objectives, whereas countries with open markets only require on average $2.40 per capita to reach the same objectives.

The wide range of values obtained within each group may be due in part to differences in GDP per capita and degree of urbanization among the countries, particularly in the case of the very poor, which

---

[112] Europe and Central Asia
[113] Middle East and North Africa

still require high levels of investment even at high degrees of liberalization. However, the correlation between the cost of achieving universal access and the degree of liberalization remains significant to warrant attention and is evidence to the point made elsewhere in this paper that liberalization is one of the most powerful vehicles to achieve universal access.

APPLICATION TO SPECIFIC COUNTRY SITUATIONS

When preparing country-specific solutions, the definition and unit costs of universal access used in this analysis need to be adapted in accordance with many country-specific factors. The following is a non-exhaustive list of such factors with proposals as to how to take them into account in the calculations[114]:

- The overall level of economic development will have an impact on the affordability of service, therefore the universal access targets will have to be revised, as mentioned above. If, for instance in Latin America, we double the targets to 1 telephone per every 500 rural inhabitants and one telecenter for every 25,000 people, the total external finance required by the sample countries in the region is multiplied by 10, and three new countries now make the list of those that need assistance: Bolivia, Ecuador and El Salvador. Similarly for ECA, where, under such targets, Russia and Bulgaria now would require external support.
- The average size of villages (or clusters of villages, if appropriate) needs to be taken into account. For instance, in Tanzania the average size of a single village is 2,500 inhabitants, while in India the average size is 1,000 inhabitants. The ratio of actual average size to the notional size of 1,000 can be used to fine-tune the cost estimates for basic telephony presented in the table.
- The level of access to telecommunications services at the village and urban center level also needs to be taken into account. For instance, in Tanzania very few villages have even a single phone, while in India about half have a phone. The cost estimates can be further fine-tuned by proportionately deducting the portion that would correspond to already served villages. Similarly for telecenters, if many urban areas already have access to such facilities.
- Existence of access to power at the village level will have an impact on the cost of the equipment. This factor can be taken into account by marking up the cost (e.g. by a factor of 2) for the proportionate number of communities that do not have access to power.
- Average distance (either by foot or by the most common local form of transport) to the nearest phone needs to be considered when defining the appropriate UA target, to ensure it is reasonable. If the local population density, average household size and the average geographical size of villages allow for clustering of several nearby villages without too adversely affecting this distance factor, one could use the average population of such clusters, instead of individual villages, in the above calculations.
- Inclusion of telecenters in the universal access definition needs to be critically assessed, and may not be appropriate in all cases (a separate funding mechanism could be envisioned, for instance). In addition, the adequate level of service in a particular country will need to be refined, based, for instance, on the average size of medium urban centers.
- The expected level of subsidy required from the fund, in terms of percentage of investment costs, will have to be adjusted, based on overall capacity of the market to attract private finance and overall foreseen profitability of the operations.

---

[114] Even with these adaptations, the cost estimates continue to be rough approximations. A detailed demand study would still be required to assess appropriate level of access, pinpoint specific locations and better evaluate cost, based on a broader base of parameters than those used in this simple methodology.

Table A-5.1. Analysis of universal access costs in 62 sample countries

Country	Teledensity 1999			Population million	Rural pop % of total	USL M$ 1% of rev.	CAPEX for UA inst. M$			Years to cover CAPEX			5 year gap M$
	Mobile	Mainline	Total				Tel.	Internet	Total	Tel.	Internet	Total	
Australia	34.22	52.00	86.22	19.0	15	140	14	19	33	0.1	0.1	0.1	0
Canada	22.66	65.50	88.16	30.5	23	190	35	31	65	0.1	0.1	0.2	0
Finland	64.97	55.20	120.17	5.2	34	40	9	5	14	0.1	0.1	0.2	0
Greece	31.13	52.80	83.93	10.6	40	37	21	11	32	0.3	0.2	0.5	0
New Zealand	12.01	49.00	61.01	3.8	14	18	3	4	7	0.1	0.1	0.2	0
United Kingdom	46.36	57.50	103.86	58.7	11	530	31	59	90	0.0	0.1	0.1	0
United States	30.66	68.20	98.86	276.0	23	2690	319	276	595	0.1	0.1	0.1	0
Total sample Advanced Countries			97.71	403.8	22	3645	433	404	837			0.1	0
Angola	0.19	0.77	0.96	12.5	67	1	40	13	53	21.0	6.5	27.5	26
Botswana	6.11	7.51	13.62	1.6	50	1	4	2	6	2.6	1.0	3.6	0
Burkina Faso	0.04	0.40	0.44	11.6	78	1	44	12	56	49.4	12.9	62.3	31
Chad	0.00	0.13	0.13	7.5	77	0	28	7	35	93.3	24.9	118.1	20
Côte d'Ivoire	1.77	1.50	3.27	14.5	58	4	42	15	56	5.9	2.1	8.0	13
Gabon	0.74	3.17	3.91	1.2	21	1	1	1	2	0.9	0.9	1.9	0
Gambia	0.42	2.30	2.72	1.3	68	0	4	1	5	14.8	4.5	19.3	2
Ghana	0.44	0.80	1.24	19.7	60	2	57	20	77	20.2	6.9	27.1	38
Kenya	0.08	1.03	1.11	29.5	68	3	99	30	128	18.7	5.6	24.2	61
Madagascar	0.18	0.32	0.50	15.5	68	1	52	16	68	57.5	17.1	74.6	38
Malawi	0.21	0.38	0.59	10.6	78	0	41	11	52	74.4	19.3	93.7	29
Mali	0.05	0.25	0.30	11.0	69	1	37	11	48	36.8	11.0	47.8	26
Mauritania	0.00	0.64	0.64	2.6	45	0	6	3	8	11.9	5.5	17.4	4
Mozambique	0.06	0.40	0.46	19.3	56	1	53	19	72	42.9	15.6	58.5	40
Niger	0.00	0.17	0.17	10.4	81	0	41	10	51	111.2	28.4	139.5	30
Nigeria	0.02	0.38	0.40	109.0	66	15	349	109	458	14.0	4.4	18.3	200
Senegal	0.95	1.79	2.74	9.2	54	2	24	9	34	9.5	3.6	13.0	12
South Africa	12.03	13.80	25.83	39.9	51	39	104	40	143	1.6	0.6	2.2	0
Tanzania	0.16	0.45	0.61	32.8	70	1	112	33	144	53.2	15.6	68.8	80
Togo	0.38	0.84	1.22	4.5	69	0	15	5	20	19.6	5.9	25.5	9
Uganda	0.26	0.26	0.52	21.6	86	1	90	22	112	62.2	14.9	77.1	63
Total Africa sample countries			3.42	385.8	66	74	1243	386	1629			13.2	722
Bangladesh	0.12	0.34	0.46	127.0	77	3	481	127	608	113.2	29.9	143.1	352
China	3.41	8.58	11.99	1270.0	68	337	4277	1270	5547	7.6	2.3	9.9	1643
India	0.19	2.65	2.84	998.0	72	36	3539	998	4537	58.2	16.4	74.6	2539
Indonesia	1.07	2.90	3.97	209.0	61	17	623	209	832	22.4	7.5	29.9	416
Malaysia	14.40	20.30	34.70	21.8	45	25	49	22	71	1.2	0.5	1.7	0
Nepal	0.02	1.13	1.15	22.4	93	1	101	22	124	89.7	19.8	109.5	71
Philippines	2.97	3.88	6.85	74.5	43	20	158	75	232	4.7	2.2	7.0	39
Sri Lanka	1.23	3.64	4.87	18.6	78	3	72	19	91	13.9	3.6	17.4	39
Thailand	3.84	8.57	12.41	60.9	78	18	236	61	297	7.7	2.0	9.7	87
Total Asia sample countries			7.53	2802.2	69	460	9536	2802	12339			16.1	5186
Bulgaria	4.23	35.40	39.63	8.3	31	4	13	8	21	2.0	1.3	3.3	0
Georgia	1.88	12.30	14.18	5.5	40	0	11	5	16	17.8	8.9	26.6	8
Hungary	16.28	37.10	53.38	10.0	36	25	18	10	28	0.4	0.2	0.7	0
Kyrgyz Rep.	0.00	7.62	7.62	4.7	68	0	16	5	21	41.5	12.2	53.7	11
Latvia	11.23	30.00	41.23	2.4	31	2	4	2	6	1.2	0.8	2.0	0
Poland	10.41	26.30	36.71	38.7	35	30	68	39	107	1.4	0.8	2.1	0
Romania	6.04	16.70	22.74	22.4	44	8	50	22	72	3.9	1.8	5.7	5
Russian fed.	1.26	21.00	22.26	147.0	23	41	169	147	316	2.5	2.1	4.6	0
Slovak Republic	17.07	30.80	47.87	5.4	43	4	12	5	17	1.6	0.7	2.3	0
Jordan	1.82	8.72	10.54	6.5	20	2	6	6	13	1.5	1.6	3.1	0
Morocco	1.34	5.26	6.60	27.9	46	9	63	28	91	4.4	1.9	6.3	11
Total ECA & MNA sample countries			24.35	278.7	31	126	430	279	708			3.4	36
Argentina	12.11	20.10	32.21	36.6	11	66	19	37	56	0.2	0.3	0.5	0
Bolivia	6.17	6.17	12.34	8.1	39	4	15	8	24	2.2	1.2	3.4	0
Brazil	8.96	14.90	23.86	168.0	20	200	165	168	333	0.5	0.5	1.0	0
Chile	14.89	20.70	35.59	15.0	15	24	11	15	26	0.3	0.4	0.7	0
Colombia	9.05	16.00	25.05	41.6	28	39	55	42	97	0.8	0.6	1.5	0
Dominican Rep.	5.13	9.81	14.94	8.4	36	6	15	8	23	1.6	0.9	2.5	0
Ecuador	4.13	9.10	13.23	12.4	37	5	22	12	35	3.0	1.6	4.6	0
El Salvador	8.41	7.60	16.01	6.2	54	4	16	6	22	2.8	1.0	3.8	0
Guatemala	3.05	5.50	8.55	11.1	61	5	33	11	44	3.9	1.3	5.3	1
Honduras	2.49	4.42	6.91	6.3	49	2	15	6	22	4.7	1.9	6.6	3
Mexico	7.80	11.20	19.00	97.4	26	90	124	97	221	0.8	0.6	1.5	0
Nicaragua	0.89	3.04	3.93	4.9	46	1	11	5	16	7.1	3.3	10.4	5
Peru	4.13	6.69	10.82	25.2	28	15	35	25	60	1.4	1.0	2.4	0
Venezuela, R.B.	14.55	10.90	25.45	23.7	14	22	16	24	40	0.4	0.6	1.1	0
Total Latin America sample countries			21.80	464.9	24	481	552	465	1017			1.3	9
Grand Total sample countries			18.17	4335.4	57		12194	4335	16529			2.1	5953

Source: ITU, World Bank, authors' estimates

Table A-5.2. Universal Access costs on a per capita basis by country groups

Country	GDP/capita 1999 (US$)	Cost (US$) UA / head
Monopoly stage		
Gambia	284	4.30
Nepal	222	5.53
Nicaragua	459	3.16
Average		*5.06*
Only cellular competition		
Greece	11,772	3.00
Botswana	3,125	3.48
Burkina Faso	222	4.82
Chad	180	4.75
Côte d'Ivoire	818	3.86
Gabon	3,999	2.02
Kenya	309	4.35
Malawi	171	4.86
Mozambique	209	3.74
Niger	171	4.92
Senegal	512	3.64
South Africa	2,969	3.60
Bulgaria	1,495	2.55
Hungary	4,730	2.84
Latvia	2,545	2.56
Romania	1,519	3.23
Slovak Republic	3,652	3.14
Ecuador	1,620	2.80
Jordan	1,150	1.95
Morocco	1,256	3.26
Average		*3.64*
Partial liberalization in fixed services		
Angola	620	4.22
Ghana	372	3.92
Mali	246	4.35
Mauritania	368	3.18
Nigeria	551	4.20
Tanzania	263	4.40
Togo	316	4.35
Bangladesh	279	4.79
China	782	4.37
India	435	4.55
Indonesia	675	3.98
Sri Lanka	846	4.89
Thailand	2,038	4.88
Kyrgyz Rep.	265	4.39
Poland	4,012	2.76
Russian Fed.	1,254	2.15
Bolivia	1,027	2.89
Brazil	3,160	1.98
Honduras	853	3.40
Venezuela, R.B.	4,312	1.67
Average		*4.15*
Average excluding India and China		*3.48*

Country	GDP/capita 1999 (US$)	Cost (US$) UA / head
Open market		
Australia	20,805	1.75
Canada	21,083	2.14
Finland	24,868	2.69
New Zealand	13,964	1.71
United Kingdom	24,168	1.54
United States	34,102	2.16
Madagascar	240	4.37
Uganda	284	5.18
Malaysia	3,607	3.24
Philippines	1,030	3.11
Georgia	526	3.01
Argentina	7,731	1.53
Chile	4,492	1.73
Colombia	2,246	2.32
Dominican Rep.	2,080	2.79
El Salvador	2,011	3.65
Guatemala	1,630	3.95
Mexico	4,966	2.27
Peru	2,267	2.38
Average		*2.40*

	Cost (US$)
Average Advanced Countries	2.07
Average Africa sample	4.22
Average Asia sample	4.40
Average ECA & MNA sample	2.54
Average Latin America sample	2.19
Average all sample countries	3.81

Source: ITU, World Bank, authors' estimates

REFERENCES

Analysys: *USO in a competitive telecoms environment*, 1997

Analysys: *The future of universal service in telecommunications in Europe*, 1997

Bhatnagar, Shubash and Rob Schware: *Information and Communication Technology in Rural Developmet – Case studies from India*, WBI Working Paper, World Bank, 2000

BMI: *Techknowledge communication handbook*, South Africa, 1999.

Cannock, Geoffrey: *Telecom Subsidies: Output-Based Contracts for Rural Services in Peru*, Viewpoint Note 234, World Bank, June, 2001

CIDA discussion paper: *Global Knowledge Partnership: A practical framework for partnering rural access*. Aug 1999.

Ernberg, Johan (ITU): *Universal access for rural development, from action to strategies*, Seminar on Multipurpose Community telecentres in Hungary, Dec 1998

Forestier, Emmanuel, Jeremy Grace and Charles Kenny: *Can Information and Communication Technologies be Pro-Poor?* World Bank, 2001

Gómez, Ricardo and Patrik Hunt: *Telecentre evaluation –A Global Perspective*. Report on International Meeting on Telecenter Evaluation, IDRC, Sept 1999

InfoDev: *Information service Centers , a partnership between businesses and NGO's: the Ghana case*, Preliminary survey for the African Poverty Reduction Network and the World Bank, April 1997

InfoDev, UNECA: *Internet economic toolkit for African policymakers*, World Bank, 1999

ITU: *Mobile Cellular,* World Telecommunication Development Report 1999

ITU: *Universal Access,* World Telecommunication Development Report 1998

ITU: *General Trends in Telecommunication Reform*, 1998

ITU: *Handbook of new developments in rural telecommunications*, 1998

Kayani, Rogati and Andrew Dymond: *Options for Rural Telecommunications Development*, World Bank Technical Paper No. 359, 1997.

Klein, Michael: *Bidding for Concessions – The impact of contract design*, Viewpoint Note 158, World Bank, November 1998

Laffont, Jean-Jacques and Jean Tirole: *Competition in telecommunications*, MIT Press, 2000

Lawson, Cina and Natalie Meyenn: *Bringing Cellular Phone Service to Rural Areas: Grameen Telecom and village pay phones in Bangladesh*, Viewpoint Note 205, World Bank, March, 2000

Mansell, Robin: *GAIT (Global Access to Information and Communication Technologies) – Priorities for action*, IDRC, July 1999

Mustafa, Laidlaw, Brand: *Telecommunications policies for Sub-Saharan Africa*, World Bank Discussion Paper, 1997

NTCA: *Initial lessons learned about private participation in telecenter development*, 2000

No-Frills Consultants: *Rural telecommunications in Nepal, A socio-economic impact study*, 1998

OECD: *Communications outlook 1999*

OFTEL: *Universal telecommunication services. Proposed arrangements for Universal Service in the UK from 1997*, Consultative Document, UK, 1996

OFTEL: *Universal Telecommunication Services –Consultation*, July 1999

OSIPTEL: *El Acceso Universal y la política del FITEL*, Peru, 1999

Ovum: *Universal Service Funding: World Best practices*, 1999

Proenza, Francisco: *Telecenter sustainability – myths and opportunities*, FAO-IADB Cooperative Program, 2001.

Pouliquen, Louis: *Rural infrastructure from a World Bank perspective*, Rural Development, World Bank, 1999

Saunders, Warford & Wellenius, *Telecommunications and Economic Development*, World Bank, Washington DC, 1994

TeleCommons Development Group, *Rural Access to ICTs – The challenge for Africa*, 2000

Townsend, David: *Telecentre implementation plan. Report to the Universal Service Agency and the Department of Communications Republic of South Africa*, 1999

Valletti, Tommaso and Antonio Estache: *The theory of access pricing: an overview for infrastructure regulators*, Policy Research Paper, World Bank Institute, 1999

Wallsten: *An empirical analysis of competition, privatization, and regulation in Africa and Latin America*, May 1999

Wellenius, Björn: *Closing the gap in access to rural communication: Chile 1995-2002*, World Bank Discussion Paper No. 430, 2002. Also available online at www.infodev.org

Wellenius, Björn: *Extending telecommunications beyond the market: towards universal service in competitive environments*, Viewpoint Note 206, World Bank, March 2000

Wellenius, Björn: *Extending Telecommunications Service to Rural Areas—The Chilean Experience: Awarding subsidies through competitive bidding*, Viewpoint Note 105, World Bank, February, 1997

World Bank: *Sector Strategy Paper – Information and Communications Technologies*, September, 2001

World Bank: *Knowledge for Development*, 1998/99 World Development Report